QUAKER QUICKS

Quakers in Politics

QUAKER QUICKS

Quakers in Politics

Margery Post Abbott

Carl Abbott

CHRISTIAN ALTERNATIVE
BOOKS

Winchester, UK
Washington, USA

JOHN HUNT PUBLISHING

First published by Christian Alternative Books, 2023
Christian Alternative Books is an imprint of John Hunt Publishing Ltd.,
No. 3 East St., Alresford, Hampshire SO24 9EE, UK
office@jhpbooks.com
www.johnhuntpublishing.com
www.christian-alternative.com

For distributor details and how to order please visit the 'Ordering' section on our website.

ISBN: 978 1 78279 420 2
978 1 78279 462 2 (ebook)
Library of Congress Control Number: 2022931608

Design: Stuart Davies

UK: Printed and bound by CPI Group (UK) Ltd, Croydon, CR0 4YY
US: Printed and bound by Thomson-Shore, 7300 West Joy Road, Dexter, MI 48130

We operate a distinctive and ethical publishing philosophy in
all areas of our business, from our global network of authors to
production and worldwide distribution.

Contents

Acknowledgments

We appreciate close readings by Deanne Butterfield, Eddy Crouch, and Lon Fendall in the United States and Michael Bartlet and John Lampen in Britain. They have helped clarify our argument and saved us from mistakes. We also have benefitted from our Quaker communities in Portland, Oregon, whose members have offered valuable feedback. Friends whom we interviewed not only shared their thoughts over Zoom but also took the time to amplify and clarify their comments. Nozizwe Madlala-Routledge and Jeremy Routledge kindly reviewed our discussion of African Friends.

Introduction

We seek a world free of war and the threat of war.
We seek a society with equity and justice for all.
We seek a community where every person's potential may be fulfilled.
We seek an earth restored.

This statement from Friends Committee on National Legislation (FCNL), based on Capitol Hill in Washington, DC, is a succinct expression of Quaker testimonies for the twenty-first century. The "we seeks" represent Quaker goals for a more just society that have developed over 370 years as Quakers have sometimes been in the vanguard of change and sometimes responded to broader historical currents. Across the Atlantic, Quaker Peace and Social Witness of Britain Yearly Meeting echoes these sentiments, writing that "people who experience Quaker worship often feel inspired to try and make the world a better place. In recognising that there is something holy in all people, Quakers recognise that all struggles and joys are connected."[1]

Writing this book has generated interesting conversations in the Abbott household, starting with the title and our understandings of the word politics. Our initial working title was *Quakers and Politics*, which places Quakers as outsiders looking in at the political process. As the book took shape, however, we found ourselves most interested in Quakers who have been directly engaged in political life, becoming fully engaged in governing their communities and nations. We also hope to cover the wide range of the Religious Society of Friends in different parts of the world and from different theological orientations. It is not a surprise that generalizations about Quakers in politics are harder to support now, when Friends have spread around the world, than in 1670 when early Quakers were often imprisoned and needed to justify their faith and practices in strong statements to the English King and Parliament.

It has also become clear that we—Carl and Marge—have different working definitions of politics. Marge's experience in thinking about prophetic ministry and working across branches of Friends leads her to an expansive view that "politics" is about the ways that groups of people interact with each other and reach agreements that make it possible to live together. Carl's background as a historian and social scientist leads him to prefer a more precise, well bounded definition that focuses on directly influencing or participating in the democratic institutions of government from town councils to Parliament and Congress. Given the space constraints of this series and its goal of quick reads, the second definition will frame the book, but with room for a more expansive take. Our choice to use "Quakers in politics" rather than "Quakers and politics" reflects this decision. The tension and choice between roles as political outsider or insider is a recurring theme.

The Quaker movement arose amid the turmoil of the Civil War in England from 1642 to 1648, and in a time when there was not a clear line between church and state. The state collected tithes from everyone to support the established church, where attendance was mandatory if sometimes laxly enforced. Many participants in the war, including first-generation Quakers, hoped that victory for Parliament would usher in God's kingdom. Dashed hopes, first under the Protectorate of Oliver Cromwell in the 1650s and then the restored monarchy after 1660, led most early Quakers to turn away from utopian politics and to assert the inward reality of Christ come and coming among his people to guide individual and community action without the intervention of a priesthood or sole reliance on the Bible. At the same time, they were aware that greed and self-interest could draw individuals astray and developed the process of discernment, encouraging individuals as well as the

2

whole community to constantly ask themselves if an action was in accord with Jesus' admonitions for right behavior and care for the powerless, especially in the Sermon on the Mount, as well as the call in *Micah* to seek both justice and mercy.

A central question for this Quaker Quick is *how* members of the Religious Society of Friends have sought over the generations and seek today to build a better world. There are many rich sources from which readers can explore the evolution of the spiritual basis of Quaker testimonies, including John Lampen, *Quaker Roots and Branches* in this series.

Actions in the political realm are wide-ranging in the issues involved, beginning with Friends' reputation as a peace church, their convincement that justice and care are essential for those who are impoverished or powerless, concern for the environment, and much more. There are many ways to try to advance God's kingdom.

- Individuals and communities change themselves and their own behaviors—recycle more, drive an electric car or no automobile at all, become a vegan, give away inherited wealth so their lives better become a witness to their faith.
- People "talk" to strangers by writing letters to the local newspaper, participating in a vigil for police reform, or supporting the Quaker Grannies who poured tea for soldiers entering military bases in Australia. When a Meeting adopts and publicizes a minute that speaks to a concern or favors a particular piece of legislation, it is talking to strangers to publicize a cause and call others to action.
- Activists take direct action outside the conventional political system, sometimes involving disruptive actions such as sit-ins and sometimes civil disobedience through the deliberate violation of unjust laws or large-scale efforts to interfere with government operations, such as

the Greenham Common Women's Peace Camp that fought the placement of nuclear-armed cruise missiles in Britain.

- Groups and individuals lobby elected and appointed officials through direct contact, trying to shape legislation, international agreements, and choices about implementing formal policies.
- Individuals serve in government itself as administrators with policy making authority and stand for elective offices as — that dreaded word — politicians.

This list of actions divides into two parts. The first three points describe individuals or Meetings acting essentially as outsiders to the political process. The last two highlight work inside the halls of politics, from sitting down with a member of Congress in her office to staffing the Quaker United Nations Office to being a genuine insider by serving in the British Cabinet like John Bright and or being President of the United States like Herbert Hoover and, yes, Richard Nixon. We can think of political action as a pyramid with a broad base of individual and group participation and advocacy that supports a narrower apex of lobbying and electoral politics. "Insiders" at the "top" face different pressures and constraints than do the "outsiders" who support them.

This second part is where we focus. We argue that Quakers have been and should be engaged in politics. We explore times and ways in which Friends have been directly involved in electoral politics, ways in which they have directly addressed kings and legislatures, from Margaret Fell in 1660 to the present, and ways in which they have helped to organize broad reform movements that press for legislative solutions. Quakers can bring something unusual to the antagonistic world of politics as bridge-builders who try to work across political divides.

"Quaker in politics" is a term with soft boundaries. Our focus is individuals whose political careers coincided with

4

active identification and involvement with the Society of Friends. Some are lifelong Quakers; others came to Friends as adults, often via connections made during political activism. We are less interested in people who came from a Quaker family and upbringing, but who were not active as adults, with the inevitable exception of Richard Nixon. We also describe explicitly Quaker organizations dedicated to lobbying and influencing public policy decisions.

We highlight individual stories and insights while looking for broader patterns and suggestions about the challenges and possibilities of Friendly politics. When we began this project, we had a shortlist of prominent Friends whom we discuss in Chapter 4. Not surprisingly, the deeper one digs, the more Quakers in politics one finds. John Bright is a prominent figure in British history, but more than thirty other Quakers served in Victorian Parliaments, most of them backbenchers who made speeches about favorite causes but didn't make it into the history books. Hundreds of Friends have served their communities in national legislatures and assemblies, in the legislative bodies of Australian and American states, and on city, borough, and regional councils in countries around the world. We have sought out the insights of several of these folks, and we hope that our book can acknowledge and support their service. There are also limitations that we want to acknowledge. First, our examples and analysis are all drawn from nations with functioning democratic governments. Second, we have not had the resources for direct research about Friends in East Africa, leaving coverage far thinner than we would like.

Both of us have worked directly with campaigns for progressive causes and progressive candidates and Marge has worked as assistant to a state legislator. We have been involved with Friends Committee on National Legislation, particularly Marge who has served as clerk of the Executive and General Committees. We believe that it is important that there be Quaker

5

voices inside the political process as well as outside, and we address both the pitfalls and promise of being a "political Quaker."

Chapter 1

A Quaker Approach to Politics

Quakers around the world have many distinct traditions and styles for living out their faith. Some Friends, as Quakers often call themselves, may define their faith in terms of political activism. Others steer away from secular engagement and, depending on their community, see themselves as mystics or declare that salvation of souls rather than political action is central to their faith community.

Yet Quakers carry within themselves as individuals and as a community a vision of God's Kingdom as the Peaceable Kingdom—what can also be called the New Creation or the City of God. Thus, amidst all their differences and strong disagreements, significant numbers of Friends long for a world where people care for the environment that sustains us, that prioritizes justice and care for the weak, teaches non-violent resolution of differences and are otherwise obedient to divine guidance.

This vision of the world as it might be may sound naïve and foolish amid threats facing the world today—but it arose in the earliest years of Quakerism—the grim middle years of the seventeenth century. Not only did the plague sweep through England, the home of early Friends; Civil War raged, the monarchy was toppled, and then restored. Much of London burned to the ground. These were not promising conditions for a good life. Yet early Friends saw themselves as living in the Kingdom of God, a kingdom that is both come and coming: a vision of the world realized as each person lives out God's will day to day yet will be realized in full at some future time. In this they differed from Puritan Calvinists who believed salvation was only for the few and who saw the Kingdom of God as solely dependent on the future arrival of Christ.

Friends have always believed, and know deep within, that the Peaceable Kingdom begins now, and it is the responsibility of everyone to live it out, to live it into being. The varied Quaker communities may express their hopes differently and at times disagree strongly on what constitutes the City of God, but most can point to a common heritage. Most affirm the words of George Fox who in the seventeenth century famously proclaimed that having come to know and be transformed by the Spirit of God amongst us, each person might become a pattern and example for others and come to walk cheerfully over the earth answering that of God in every person.

In 1659, Edward Burrough wrote a clear statement of Quaker engagement in politics, saying: "We are not for names, nor men, nor titles of Government, nor are we for this party or against the other ... but we are for justice and mercy and truth and peace and true freedom, that these may be exalted in our nation, and that goodness, righteousness, meekness, temperance, peace and unity with God, and with one another, that these things may abound." He laid out many of the principles that shape Quaker action down to the twenty-first century, principles that draw on the Sermon on the Mount and its call to love one's enemies; other passages echo the call in Galatians and in the epistle of James to reject arrogance, greed, selfishness, and the desire for revenge. Twisting facts or degrading the reputation of others are antithetical to the teaching of Jesus and remain central to the guidance of the Holy Spirit today.

Such principles apply to every aspect of life and are not limited to the pages of a single book. Quakers encourage one another to listen inwardly for this divine guidance and how it remains vital even as circumstances change. At their best, Friends who pay attention to this inward guide approach the political realm with fresh eyes and an openness to creative solutions.

Quakers, like anyone immersed in electoral politics constantly come face-to-face with pressures for compromise and demands for effectiveness. It is important that Friends are clear and open when they do accept partial solutions or results. Individuals find their own answers in the realities of seeking election and working for just legislation while sustaining a clear sense of integrity. Taking an absolute stance may leave much damage. The Friends Service Committee in Britain refused to lobby to improve conditions for young men who had been imprisoned for refusing to fight during World War I, believing it was unethical to lobby for Quakers without working on behalf of all objectors to fighting. Many young men suffered greatly.

Quakers affirm the centrality of truth and integrity in politics, and at the same time, note the complexity of adhering to truth in the political realm. Jo Vallentine, who served in the Australian Senate, stated in a lecture to Australian Friends at their annual gathering:

> It is the never-ending and often frustrating search for truth which is a constant motivation in my work for peace. An informed public, in a democracy, will usually make sensible decisions for the general well-being. Unfortunately, it is in the interest of the few to control the masses by keeping them uninformed, and therefore unable to contribute as intelligently as they would like, to the decision-making processes. It is the age old 'mushroom treatment' – keep the populace in the dark and feed them manure, to put it politely![2]

Quakers and other people of faith who participate actively in politics can see themselves as engaged in what historian and theologian Martin Marty first described as public theology. They bring their religious values and convictions into dialogue with wider publics, not to press a single solution but to explore how different publics and communities can come to understand common paths forward. At its best, it is an approach that is committed to fundamental moral values but not absolutist, one that listens much more than it preaches.

Activists and scholars have drawn inspiration from Quaker efforts to mend the social fabric, particularly from their experiences at peacemaking, mediation, and reconciliation in civil conflicts in places such as Bosnia, Nigeria, Northern Ireland, and South Africa. Books by Adan Curle, C. H. Mike Yarrow, H. W. van der Merwe, Sydney Bailey, and Andrew Rigby draw principles from this work. Their analysis can be supplemented by the work of Elise Boulding on the importance of building a consensus-seeking culture through nongovernmental organizations and George Lakey's practical theorizing from decades of work with the Movement for a New Society in the United States. A common theme is the importance for each party in conflict to acknowledge the humanity of the others, a point we reiterate about the formal political process as well. Successful mediation starts with building relationships before addressing concrete questions. Friends can bring a patient ministry of presence and practice the values that are the intended outcome, expecting the spiritual to inform the practical.

Sometimes the pragmatism of the political life often seems the opposite of the call to prophetic ministry that is a distinctive feature of Quaker faith and practice. Jo Vallentine, along with many other Friends, values transparency in their actions and in the positions they take on issues even as they may differ in their conclusions: how does one weigh the importance of the testimony against war when war is being fought to end slavery? Is nuclear deterrence a valid means of maintaining peace in the world in midst of Cold War? There are many such questions that have tempered Quaker adherence to their testimonies when they are in apparent conflict. As there is no body that can make and enforce decisions on behalf of all Friends worldwide, answers from individuals, congregations, and regional or national bodies may vary significantly, although Friends Service Committees in Canada, Britain and elsewhere or Friends Committee on National Legislation in the United States can speak on behalf of significant numbers of Friends because of the consultative process that informs their actions.

What might Quaker political action look like in practice in the twenty-first century?

In December 2007 Kenya experienced devastating violence during its national elections. Kenyan Quakers wasted no time in making a powerful statement to Kenya's President setting out Quaker principles and proposing a way forward for the nation. Friends actively sought to change public policy even as they were working to ameliorate the conditions of Internally Displaced Persons who had lost their homes in the violence and encouraging wide use of cell phones to help quell the ongoing street violence. The Kenyan statement has similarities to one made in England 1661 by Margaret Fell, and other influential Friends, addressing the King and Parliament regarding Quaker principles and the importance of non-violence.

Esther Mombo and Cecile Nyiramana offer context for the Quaker response to the violence in Kenya following the 2007 elections, noting multiple factors contributing to the election hostilities and the need to actively break down the distrust which permeates Kenyan politics. While by no means free of problems related to tribalism and patriarchy, Quakers have gained a reputation for integrity and a willingness to engage in addressing the root causes of long-standing injustices. They have learned that sustainable work in shifting from a culture of violence to one of peacebuilding requires a holistic approach to conflict that addresses ethical and religious as well as economic issues. Women have taken on significant leadership in programs aimed at healing the wounds of violence and its effects on the political and religious dimensions of Kenyan life. Including all stakeholders in a process that traditionally was the provenance of powerful men is also essential to lasting change.

Peacebuilding in Kenya

"In Kenya the boundaries have remained the same in post-colonial times as they were in colonial times. The colonial boundaries reflected both ethnic and denominational segregation ... [which] feeds into negative and power politics when politicians capitalize on exclusion and marginalization. The 'us and them' political syndrome that brings about divisions based on a negative view of the other encourages animosity and lack of trust of the other. The other is portrayed as that which will take over and rule in a terrible way. The other is portrayed as one who will not share resources; the other is portrayed as evil. In this situation the youth are manipulated and used to fight each other rather than being encouraged to ask questions of the politicians about what structural plans they have for enhancing growth.

When peacebuilders address the root causes of these issues, they can help people to better understand the dynamics of conflicts. In doing this, one does not shy away from naming the historical grievances around the cultural tensions that continue to rock communities. In addressing the legacies of historical injustice peacebuilders are engaged in deeper dialogue about recurring intergroup tensions and are rebuilding trust."[3]

The history of silent, expectant waiting as central to Friends ways of worship has the perhaps unexpected benefit in the busy-ness of modern life that it is very portable and requires no special venues or symbols. Small groups of Quakers might stand in the halls of the US Senate office building and settle into a period of quiet attention to the inward voice of the Holy Spirit as they gather for a lobby visit or find themselves in extended worship as part of deciding their national corporate priorities for action.

Conversations with Quakers who have been active lobbyists or who have been elected to public office keep coming back to several themes, which we explore more fully in the final chapter. We share Catherine West's belief that Quakers have something to offer the political process, and at our best bring principles and concerns to bear in open dialogue with people who may or may not agree. Speak truth. Listen to other people's stories as well as telling our own. Let go of the demands of ego. Build relationships. A Quaker lobbyist often needs to approach legislators and their staff with a sense of curiosity and a willingness to understand the human reality that can open up seemingly intractable differences. The same is just as true for Quakers who serve in elective office. In sharing the stories that bring alive the ways in which decisions affect individuals, a lobbying session can become a time for problem-solving and building relationships which benefit a larger portion of the constituency involved than a simple party line approach. As Marian Hobbs, a former Labour Party member in the New Zealand Parliament said when we spoke with her in 2021 "the Quaker approach to politics is not so much about what, as how."

Humility is another dimension that stands out in the egocentric political arena. A true intent to improve people's lives can cut through at least some of the distrust and hostility that is often prevalent in politics. As one Quaker legislator noted, what she brought to the job is what got her elected. People could trust what she said knowing that she was not taking the work on for personal gain. DeAnne Butterfield reports that the Governor of Colorado hired her to promote his goals in the state legislature because she was a Quaker and he wanted to move beyond what had become a very contentious relationship. He understood that Friends bring a gift to politics — the gift of seeing that there may be more than two answers to a problem. The yes/no, either/or mindset can paralyze public life as two sides entrench their positions. The Quaker approach has the potential to begin to untie the knotted process. Carefully working to untangle the different strands rather than trying to slice through with a single stroke may be slower but more productive. The willingness of Quakers to be open about the values that underpin their work gives a model of politics that aims at caring for those without power or resources and seeking actions that encourage stewardship of creation.

This approach to politics has many similarities with a call to prophetic ministry, and in fact, it is not unusual to encounter individuals who describe their work as a ministry and find at times that their willingness to listen for the work of the Spirit in some of the most contentious political situations is to provide a real service to all those involved.

One way to describe Quakers is as a band of everyday prophets. This is NOT talking about foretelling the future! Nor is it about being focused on and constantly upset by the nightly news. Everyday prophets are people (whether they call themselves Quaker or not) who listen deep within for divine guidance that points toward compassion, toward justice, toward generosity and an abundant peace. The everyday prophet seeks to pay regular attention to this inward Light guiding them through the constant, ordinary pressures to focus on success, wealth, greed, and arrogance, to act on that guidance. The four "we seeks" which begin this book are reminders of the world Friends strive to be part of and to make a reality.

While a few people experience a calling that throws their life upside down, often an individual will be nudged to take an action that is neither dramatic nor even very visible. Here I think of our friend Rachel Cunliffe, who for many years worked to end the death penalty, then realized an important part of her calling was to sit with people and listen to them. This included the families of victims as you might imagine, but also those on death row, and even the law enforcement officers, the defense attorneys and all those who were entangled in the criminal justice system. She served as a minister to them as well, seeking to make visible and nurture the light of God within each of them.

The everyday prophet lives to the best of their capacity in accord with what the Inward Light shows them and seeks to make that Inward Teacher available to others. To say this another way:

Discernment is central: Can I sort out my motivations and see what is of God and what comes from ambition or fear? Do I recognize the sources of the various voices in my head pushing me to sometimes contradictory actions?

Once I hear what the inward Light might be telling me, am I willing to act?

Then, as I look at the world around me, can I see what is Life-giving and draw it out in others?

The community of Friends not only carries within itself a vision of a world, but Friends also hold time-tested practices for personal discernment and group decision-making which help us as we seek to live out that vision. Paul Buckley reminds us in a very practical way, that we have to be willing to do our best to follow divine guidance, then perhaps to fail, then try again, make mistakes and seek out those who can help us improve, just as if we were part of a baseball team — we cannot hit a home run every time at bat. Not even the greatest football players (that's soccer for you Americans) score in every match or save every shot on goal.

This community of everyday prophets recognizes that being a Friend is not a solitary exercise, but rather a body of people committed to helping one another listen better, and practice, and hold one another up when inevitably we fall. Together, the prophetic community speaks of hope, sharing what it is like to be filled with the Spirit despite the many times when disagreements and personality clashes seem to prevail. The hope is for a community that carries with it an awareness of the divine spark in each human person, a spark which resists being driven by fear or dominated by self-will. The prophetic calling is about speaking truth, boldly yet with respect.

The title of Quaker Anna Fritz's song "I Hold You Up" is a reminder of the importance of developing relationships in the work of politics.

I hold you up in the light of God.
I hold you up in my own heart.
I hold you up in the healing light.
I hold you up 'cause the time is right.[4]

Friends have always believed, and know deep within, that the Peaceable Kingdom begins now, and it is our responsibility to live it out, to live it into being. George Fox famously proclaimed that having come to know and be transformed by the Spirit of God amongst us, we might become patterns and examples for others and come to walk cheerfully over the earth answering that of God in very person.

Chapter 2

The First Century: In the World or Apart?

The first generation of Quakers faced a dilemma. Could they best hasten the Kingdom of God by engaging with those who wielded political power or by surviving as a group that could set a moral example. Even George Fox was of two minds, importuning Lord Protector Oliver Cromwell by letter and face-to-face in the 1650s but urging a low profile in the 1660s after the restoration of the monarchy squashed hopes for radical political change. As members of a legally marginal minority, Fox and other Quakers opted to preserve the movement by refraining from direct political involvement except in advocating for religious toleration. By the time freedom of worship was granted in 1689, the momentum for withdrawal was strong, leading English Quakers to focus their efforts on their families, farms, and factories rather than civic life.

The Quaker movement coalesced in an environment of political turmoil where different groups and factions competed vehemently and often violently to shape the future of England. George Fox's soul-shaking experience of the healing power of the inward Christ came to him in 1647 as the long Civil War between the forces of Crown and Parliament was reaching its climax. His vision of a "great people to be gathered" to Christ that came as he preached on Pendle Hill in Lancashire came three years after Parliamentary leaders executed Charles I in an action that roiled all of Europe. The 1650s were a decade when diverse groups clamored for drastic change—a leveling of economic distinctions, abolition of a centralized church, the institution of Godly government. Oliver Cromwell kept a lid on chaotic change during the 1650s as Lord Protector. His death in 1658 briefly renewed hopes of a transformed nation—until the restoration of the monarchy with Charles II twenty-one months later put the kibosh on radical hopes. This was the political world in which tens of thousands of early Quakers made their way, and with a dramatic change in approach from the 1650s to the 1660s.

In 1659, when England again looked open to fundamental change, George Fox published *To the Parliament of the Common-Wealth of England, Fifty-nine Particulars laid down for the Regulating of things, and the taking away of Oppressing laws, and Oppressors, and to ease the Oppressed*. Fox expressed the hopes of all Quakers that they could worship as they pleased and the hopes of many of them for a more just society. The fifty-nine "particulars" (presumably keyed to the year 1659) were practical, beginning with "Let no man be prisoned for Tithes" and, continuing, nor for failing to doff his hat nor for refusing to swear oaths nor for meeting together. They were also aspirational, asking for reform of the judicial system, the distribution of church lands to the poor, the transformation of abbeys and steeple-houses into almshouses, and that "all those fines that belong to Lords of Mannors, be given to the poor people, for the Lords have enough." It was a hopeful call for a more egalitarian England that echoed what other radical Quakers had been saying, like Edward Burrough's evocation of the Godly Kingdom. "Laws and decrees shall be changed and renewed. Every yoke and burden shall be taken off from the neck of the poor; true judgment and justice, mercy and truth, peace and righteousness shall be exalted; and all the nations shall have judges as at the first and counselors as at the beginning."

Quakers in 1661 had a different dilemma. The new government was cracking down on potential opposition, looking for threats of rebellion from a heavily armed populace with lots of seasoned and disillusioned supporters of Commonwealth ideals and arresting Quakers on suspicion. Deeply worried about official repression, Fox and key Quakers including Margaret Fell decided that their best hope was to be left alone. Like Fox's *Fifty-Particulars* addressed to Parliament, a letter addressed to the throne was about as far as an ordinary person could participate in high-level politics. The Quaker leaders thus wrote the King that "we utterly deny all outward wars and strife and fightings with outward weapons, or any end or under any pretence whatsoever." The statement, which has served as the foundation of the modern Quaker peace testimony, had the practical goal of assuring the government that Quakers had no intention of getting involved in any armed resistance to the restored monarchy and, by implication, any political involvement beyond defending their own worship and practices. Alexander Parker in 1660 encapsulated this caution: "My advice and counsel is that every one of you, who love and believe in the Light, be still and quiet, and side not with any parties."

Keeping a completely apolitical profile proved impossible. The Quaker Act that went into effect in 1662 declared them to be a secret sect that posed a danger to the nation for refusing to take lawful oaths, particularly oaths of allegiance to the Crown. The law also forbade assembly in any pretense of worship by Quakers over age sixteen. Strict enforcement led to massive imprisonment. While Friends kept up a barrage of pamphlets and books defending their beliefs, an estimated 15,000 Friends suffered imprisonment and over four hundred died in jail for worshipping outside the established church and refusing to take oaths or to pay tithes to support the clergy. Around 1675, they began to actively campaign for their religious rights. Influential Friends like William Penn buttonholed Members of Parliament. The Yearly Meeting made certain that Quakers attended committee hearings and recorded every vote to track supporters and opponents, even renting a room in a coffee house close by the Houses of Parliament for a base of operations where leaders like Fox could quietly meet with Members of Parliament. Even after the Toleration Act of 1689 granted freedom of worship to all Protestants, Quakers continued to lobby until a law in 1696 allowed them to substitute a simple affirmation for a formal oath in courts and legal proceedings. However, English law continued to disqualify principled Friends from holding public office for another 110 years until the Reform Act of 1832 extended the option of affirmation.

Things began differently in North America, where New Jersey and Pennsylvania originated as Quaker colonies. The towering figure (literally in bronze atop Philadelphia city hall since 1894) was William Penn, who was politically successful because of his family, social standing, and ability to talk directly with kings, and not because of his Quaker faith. The result, of course, was the Quaker colony of Pennsylvania, granted to Penn as colonial proprietor. Under English law, colonial proprietors were granted the *English* property rights to a chunk of North America. They were expected to purchase land rights from the local Indigenous people and could then resell that land to other settlers at a markup in a giant real estate deal—so long as the French in Canada or the Spanish in Florida didn't interfere with English control. That is what William Penn got from Charles II in March 1681. In return for canceling a very substantial debt that the crown had owed to his father, a successful and prominent admiral, Penn was granted the right to claim tens of millions of acres of lands stretching westward from the west bank of the Delaware River.

Quakers were already a governmental presence in America. Beginning in the 1670s they were prominent in what is now the state of New Jersey. In 1682, while actively engaged with planning Pennsylvania, he and eleven associates bought the proprietary rights to East Jersey and encouraged Quakers to settle there; Robert Barclay, the Quaker theologian, served as governor of East Jersey and arranged the settlement of the town of Perth Amboy as its first capital. West Jersey, along the east bank of the Delaware River, was even more heavily Quaker. There were also plenty of Quakers in North Carolina, where William Archdale would serve as governor 1695–96, and in Rhode Island, which had several Quaker governors in the colonial era.

Unlike in England, Quakers in many of England's overseas colonies could hold elective office (if they were property-owning men, of course) and hold local and provincial office. Penn believed in democratic institutions, establishing and working with representative bodies even when they had minds of their own. In the Pennsylvania Charter of Privileges that he issued in 1701, he accepted limits on his personal authority, but began the document with one provision that could not be amended or removed—a confirmation of liberty of conscience to all who believed in God and pledged to "live quietly under civil government" while restricting office holding to Quakers and other Christians.

Even in Pennsylvania, trouble brewed for the connection between Quakers and politics. Not surprisingly, Penn's absence from his colony after 1701 and then his death in 1718 left openings for factions and rivalries in the colonial legislature. More importantly, the colony's remarkable prosperity and its formal religious toleration attracted far more non-Quakers than Quakers in the first half of the eighteenth century. Maintaining the essence of a Quaker experiment required acknowledgement of British authority and increasingly onerous compromises. Quakers managed to hold control of its legislative assembly to the 1740s but growing tensions with non-Quakers and newcomers went from simmer to boil in 1755. The early Pennsylvania Assembly had refused to create a militia, and it found evasive workarounds for war taxes such as voting money "for the Queen's use" even while knowing it might go to military needs. After General William Braddock's stunning defeat in western Pennsylvania at the start of the French and Indian War (Seven

Years' War), however, the Assembly's majority of non-Quakers imposed a war tax and established a militia—direct action that trumped Quaker sleight of hand. Most Friends resigned from the Assembly in 1756, leaving politically active Quakers a minority in the "Quaker colony."

Twenty years later, when most of the North American colonies chose open rebellion against British authority and declared independence, the Society adopted strict neutrality, refusing to affirm loyalty to either side. Four-fifths of eligible Quaker men refused to take up arms. Those who did join the fight defined themselves as a separate group of Free Quakers outside the formal Yearly Meeting structure. Most Quakers also declined to pay war taxes imposed by the Patriot side and many would not accept the currency issued by the Continental Congress, which amounted to the same refusal to support the rebellion financially. The costs to businesses and personal reputations were considerable. A Philadelphia mob trashed scores of Quaker homes for failure to properly celebrate the victory at Yorktown in 1781. Adherence to pacifist principles meant that members of the Society of Friends were largely sidelined from the politics of nation building in the aftermath of the Revolution.

The choice of moral uprightness over continued political involvement in 1756 was a harbinger of an "official" inward turn. In 1758 Philadelphia Yearly Meeting advised its members to "beware of accepting of, or continuing in, the exercise of any office or station in civil society or government" which required actions inconsistent with Quaker testimonies. The concern strengthened over the ensuing decades. The temptations and corruption of "the world" threatened Quaker unity and Quaker souls. Friends were expected to improve their farms, work diligently in their businesses, and attend meeting with equal diligence. North Carolina Yearly Meeting laid it on the line in 1854 and spoke for many American Friends in that century: "It is the sense of the Yearly Meeting, that if any of our members accept, or act in, the office of member of the federal or state legislature, justice of the peace, clerk of a court, coroner, sheriff, or constable, that they be dealt with, and if they cannot be convinced of the inconsistency of their conduct, after sufficient labor, they be disowned."

Something of the same thing had already happened in Britain, but earlier, meaning that the ebb and flow of political involvement had different timing on the two sides of the Atlantic. The Affirmation Act in 1722 had satisfied the compelling Quaker agenda for *religious* recognition. The Society in its third generation turned inward in what is known as the Quietist period, focusing on individual spirituality and avoiding unnecessary non-economic engagement with the larger society. Like many United States Friends in the next century, they were "resolutely oblivious" in the phrase of historian Frederick Tolles. Respected figures likened political campaigns to the opening of hell. Some even admonished against reading newspapers and against voting.

Change came after 1832. Joseph Pease became the first Quaker to serve in Parliament, against the wishes of his family and meeting. John Bright (more about him later) was the second in 1843. London Yearly Meeting continued to caution Friends about the conflicts between right practice and political responsibility, but by the mid-twentieth century more than sixty Friends had followed the lead of Pease and Bright, each of them dealing with the dilemmas of power and compromise in their own way. Substantial numbers served in the Victorian era and the Yearly Meeting endorsed standing for office in the 1911 edition of *Faith and Practice*. Quakers were also a substantial presence in Parliament in the immediate aftermath of World War II.

Chapter 3

Quakers as Reformers

Midway through the anti-slavery novel *Uncle Tom's Cabin* (1852), a Quaker farm couple in Ohio offer refuge to Eliza Harris and her son after her escape from enslavement by leaping from one "green fragment of ice" to the next to cross the floe-choked Ohio River. At the home of Simeon and Rachel Halliday she finds safety from pursuing enslavers and reunites with her husband, George Harris. Other Quakers guide the family from the safe house to a boat that takes them across Lake Erie to freedom in Canada.

Harriet Beecher Stowe's novel sold hundreds of thousands of copies in the United States and more than a million in England. Its dramatic story helped to burnish the reputation of Quakers as leaders in the battle against slavery as stalwarts of the Underground Railroad and as public voices for abolition. The public impression was correct. Quakers in the nineteenth century were adamant in opposition to slavery. It had also taken them a good while to get there. It is a good issue for exploring how a concern can progress from the personal to the political — from something that Quakers asked of themselves to something that they demanded of their nations.

Slavery was embedded in England's Caribbean and North American colonies by the time Quakers began migrating and making converts in the 1670s and 1680s. William Penn himself enslaved at least eleven individuals at his Pennsylvania estate, not unlike other wealthy Friends. Some also had ties to the trade in enslaved people. Large landowners with estates to work and shipowners looking for business had little motivation to question a practice that all their peers accepted and that benefitted them directly. Few were interested in being taken to task as enslavers.

The first anti-slavery Quakers were thus lonely voices. As early as 1688, a group of German and Dutch Quakers living in a village outside Philadelphia broadcast what is known as the Germantown Protest, the first public condemnation of slavery by white North Americans. Friends are justly proud of the Germantown Protest, but the cause was too controversial for other meetings to take up and it went nowhere—except the archives of the Haverford College Library. A generation later, Benjamin Lay was fierce and dramatic, pulling no punches in writing *All Slave-keepers that keep the Innocent in Bondage, Apostates*. He once showed up at Philadelphia Yearly Meeting dressed as a soldier, delivered an anti-slavery sermon buttressed with Bible verses, and then plunged a sword into the Bible and skewered a bladder filled with blood. The sober-sided Quakers in attendance were not amused and several meetings disowned him.

Where Benjamin Lay was fierce, John Woolman was gentle but unrelenting in laboring with Friends and others over the immorality of slaveholding. He began his anti-slavery ministry by refusing to assist in writing a will that included slaves as heritable property. Over several decades, he traveled in the ministry, visiting meetings and individuals and quietly but insistently arguing the basic immorality of human bondage. He was reserved in manner but tireless in pressing his radical arguments about the corrupting effects of slavery on everyone involved. When visiting a slave owner, he paid the slaves who served him out of his own pocket.

Woolman was also a pivotal figure, or at least his pamphlet *Some Considerations on the Keeping of Negroes, recommended to the professors of Christianity of every denomination*. In 1754, pushy younger Friends took control of Philadelphia Yearly Meeting from conservative leaders who didn't want to rock the boat. Their decision to publish Woolman's pamphlet with Yearly

Meeting endorsement began a process of internal reform that eroded and then negated the influence of wealthy slave-owning Quakers, making abolition a corporate testimony.

- Philadelphia Yearly Meeting began tentatively in 1754 by issuing its own *Epistle of Caution and Advice Concerning the Buying and Keeping of Slaves* that instructed members not to transport or sell enslaved people but did not make it a censurable offense. Three years later, it banned anyone who traded in enslaved people from leadership roles. Some meetings complied more readily than others. Wilmington Meeting in Delaware, for example, moved to disown any member who traded in slaves, and Wilmington Friends began to free their slaves in 1761.
- Nevertheless, manumission progressed slowly. Not until 1774 did Philadelphia Yearly Meeting resolve that slave owning was inconsistent with the Society of Friends and told meetings to send visiting committees to convince individual Quakers to free their slaves. Two years later the Yearly Meeting agreed to disown members who still failed to do so. The other yearly meetings from the Carolinas to New England all took the same steps by the end of the 1770s.
- The last step in corporate witness was the question of membership. Not until the mid-1790s did Philadelphia Yearly Meeting finally decide that Black people could not only worship with other Quakers but be admitted to membership (the hang-up had been fear that once a Black person was a member, a Meeting would have to be open to interracial marriages).

More importantly for a book about Quakers in politics, they also turned outward. Anthony Benezet amplified Woolman's message with *A Caution and Warning of the Calamitous State of the Enslaved Negroes* (1767), started a school for free Blacks in 1770, and was active in persuading the Pennsylvania legislature to adopt phased emancipation in 1780. Other northern states followed by 1804, influenced to varying degrees by local Friends. In 1790 Philadelphia Yearly Meeting took the further step of petitioning Congress to abolish slavery nationwide, confident that Quakers in the new nation now stood on firm moral ground. This last was a cause that was going nowhere fast because the regulation of slavery was the province of highly independent-minded states, with the federal role limited to the international trade in enslaved people.

British Quakers followed a similar path from personal to political. Quiet anti-slavery efforts among Friends themselves went public after the thirteen colonies gained independence and the northern states debated and began to eliminate slavery. London Yearly Meeting had prohibited members from engaging in the slave trade in the 1760s, but a primary goal was to maintain the moral standing of Quakers themselves. In 1783, however, David Barclay led a delegation of Quakers to urge the Board of Trade to consider anti-slavery petitions (there seems to have been a growing sense of competition between American and British Friends to demonstrate their moral standing). Four years later, nine of the twelve men who met in a London printing shop to found Britain's Abolition Society were Quakers, starting a movement that quickly grew beyond the Society of Friends but retained close ties with it.

The career of Delaware Quaker Warner Mifflin encapsulates the transition from personal to political. After coming to his own realization that he needed to free his inherited slaves in 1774, he had continued to work within the Religious Society of Friends to speed emancipation and to encourage what we can call reparations, meaning help to set former slaves up for success in freedom. He also turned to work beyond the Society of Friends. Nearby Virginia forbade manumission without explicit consent of legislature and governor, an almost impossible requirement. In 1782, Mifflin traveled extensively among Virginia Quakers to build support for easier manumission, and then he and several others spent nineteen days lobbying the Virginia Assembly. After much back and forth the Assembly received the petition, and Mifflin and other Friends had long evening talks with legislators that culminated in success. Mifflin continued to labor in Virginia, Delaware, Maryland, and North Carolina to make manumission easier, to prevent kidnapping and re-enslavement of free Blacks, and to accept a phase-out of slavery. He fine-tuned strategies making strategic alliance with groups like Methodists working behind the scenes while a prominent person was the public face for the cause.

Mifflin also went national. He helped to petition the Continental Congress to end the slave trade in 1783. He traveled with other Quakers to New York to talk directly with members of Congress, and may have had indirect influence on the Northwest Ordinance of 1787 that prohibited slavery in what would become the states of Ohio, Indiana, Illinois, Michigan, and Wisconsin. In 1790 he was back lobbying the first Congress under the new Constitution, using the well-practiced combination of presenting petitions, distributing English abolitionist Thomas Clarkson's pamphlets, and talking with individuals, even those intensely supportive of slavery. He was part of an eleven-member delegation of Quakers who launched what historian Gary Nash called "the first sustained lobbying effort in America history." Mifflin provided the first recorded oral testimony to a special committee set up to consider what Constitutional authority Congress had in relation to slavery and provided sympathetic committee members with talking points. He buttonholed Congressmen in the lobby and showed up at their lodgings for hour-long talks and arguments and even visited President Washington, hoping he'd use his influence (dropping in on the President unannounced was easier back then, and he did it more than once).

Mifflin lived a generation before abolitionism became a national political movement in which Quakers were influential but a minority. State-level emancipation stalled in the early nineteenth century when the explosive growth of cotton growing increased the demand for enslaved workers across the South. National politics polarized around the question of allowing slavery into new western states created on lands seized from Indigenous peoples — the issue that was the underlying cause of the Southern Rebellion of 1861–65.

Friends continued to balance work within the Society and outside. Quaker poet John Greenleaf Whittier was a very public Quaker. A leading literary figure (one of the founders of the *Atlantic Monthly* literary magazine) he was also an unrelenting abolitionist who was an organizer of the American Anti-Slavery Society in 1833. He edited a series of abolitionist newspapers from 1828 until 1857, calling for immediate emancipation, at some peril to himself, and published anti-slavery poems. He was a Quaker activist who was deeply engaged in politics, working to persuade sympathetic Congressmen to stand up for their principles. He helped to organize the Liberty Party in 1839 and then the Free Soil Party, some of the seeds from which the anti-slavery Republican Party of Abraham Lincoln would grow. While Whittier opted for direct political engagement, other Friends continued to work as individuals and as a religious community. Because their state prohibited manumission, for example, Quakers in North Carolina deeded enslaved individuals to the Yearly Meeting to provide de facto if not de jure freedom, which most used to move to free states.

Anti-slavery activism became intertwined with questions of women's rights at the same time that it became a national movement. Lucretia Mott was a Quaker powerhouse who traveled in the ministry, lectured wherever she could find an audience, and organized people for action. In 1833 she helped to create the Philadelphia Female Anti-Slavery Society—interracial and interdenominational but limited to one gender by social conventions. She took on peace advocacy, temperance, and the needs of Native American women in her spare time. She attended the World Anti-Slavery Convention in London in 1840, only to be denied recognition as a delegate because only men were to be seated. The experience led her to develop plans for a women's rights meeting. Working with several other Quaker women and with Elizabeth Cady Stanton, her idea culminated in what became the Seneca Falls Convention in 1848, the landmark declaration of the equal rights of women. Mott would continue tireless work for women's rights and was joined in leadership by the younger Quaker Susan B. Anthony. In 1873, Anthony was convicted of violating the law by voting in the previous election and fined $100. She assured the judge of her intent to "earnestly and persistently continue to urge all women to the practical recognition of the old revolutionary maxim that 'Resistance to tyranny is obedience to God.'" This trial marked the shift from a fight for women's rights generally to a focus on the right to vote.

Women who were anti-slavery and women's rights activists posed a dilemma for the economically successful men who controlled local and yearly meetings and accepted many prevailing social norms. Quakers had long recognized women's spiritual gifts for ministry, for example, but social custom precluded them speaking to public gatherings that were judged "promiscuous," meaning men and women in the same audience. The solution was often to speak in someone's parlor or from their front porch. Quakers may have abhorred slavery, but Quaker men could be very uncomfortable when the message was carried by fierce women such as Angelina Grimké or Abby Kelley Foster, who left the Society of Friends because stodgy and cautious meetings often refused to open meetinghouses to anti-slavery speakers. Susan B. Anthony left her original meeting to worship with a self-defined group of Progressive Friends and then with Unitarians although she retained her Quaker membership.

A half century later a similar dynamic played out when young Alice Paul, who had learned radical tactics as a participant in the Women Suffrage movement in England, returned to the United States in 1910. Quaker women had long been leaders in the North American Woman Suffrage Association—Florence Kelley, M. Carey Thomas, Marian Wright Chapman, and others following the track laid down by Susan Anthony. Hicksite yearly meetings supported the cause through their Friends Equal Rights Association. The Hicksite Philadelphia Yearly Meeting in 1914 recommended that its monthly meetings "be watchful for opportunities to influence equal suffrage legislation and encouraged their members to give active interest in the accomplishment of this reform."[5] Paul, however, found that her quiet Hicksite meeting in New Jersey did not at all approve of going to jail or breaking windows on behalf of votes for women, and she soon stepped away from active involvement with Friends, although retaining her membership. Over the next decade she honed political skills of lobbying, nonviolent protest, and political pressure. She also formed the National Woman's Party, which played a key role in passage of the Nineteenth Amendment that gave women the right to vote after its ratification in 1920 and introduced the Equal Rights Amendment (which would languish until the 1970s and still had not passed as of 2022). In the summation of historian Margaret Hope Bacon, "she took her place in a tradition of Quaker women who were so far ahead of their time that they lost patience with the Society, and yet had a major influence on later generations of Quaker women."[6]

Other women were among the early missionaries who carried Quaker faith and practice to Africa and Latin America in the late nineteenth and early twentieth centuries, including in their teaching an expectation of rights for women and their testimony to non-violence. However, Ane Marie Bak Rasmussen notes in *A History of the Quaker Movement in Africa* that these were initially instituted in relation to individual behavior rather than through legislative action and often affected by colonial rule. For instance, from the middle of the 1920s, Quakers in Kenya created their own villages which outlawed drinking, smoking and other practices associated by missionaries with pre-colonial behavior. In the 1940s the Dini ya Msambwa, a political and religious movement opposing colonial authorities, included some individuals from Quaker churches. As multiple yearly meetings were formed in East Africa, African Friends gained responsibility for their own yearly meetings about the same time as Kenyans gained national independence. The men took care to balance out different tribal interests while the women acted to form separate bodies advocating for women's interests among Friends and established a practice of bringing together women from all yearly meetings.

The Friends in this chapter were outsiders to the political system who worked to influence elected officials as well as other Quakers. These individuals always faced choices about driving forward with a cause and maintaining a purity of action or building a coalition and perhaps compromising in the process. The tension between the outsider with demands and the elected official with multiple concerns is inherent in the political process. It is the dilemmas of being a Quaker *in* politics that we begin to explore in the next chapter.

Chapter 4

Peace, War, and Friends in High Places

John Bright had a family problem. A fiercely committed social reformer with deep Quaker roots, his desire to liberalize the British economy led him into public life and then to a seat in Parliament in 1843 — the beginning of a forty-six-year run as MP. A majority of voters in Durham wanted him in Parliament, but his wife was dubious, and in-laws deeply concerned. It was commendable, they thought, for Friends to work as quiet persuaders in the manner of John Woolman or public advocates in the manner of Elizabeth Fry, but not to go over completely to the other side to become a politician. His future wife wondered whether "thy political engagement ... may not interfere with the duties of a domestic and quiet life" and his mother-in-law advised that political engagement would undermine "the meditative life of the soul." London Yearly Meeting in 1843 issued an epistle that hoped "Friends may always be found among those who are quiet in the land."

British Friends in the early nineteenth century were caught between their own desire for social reform, the earnest example of evangelical Protestants with increasing influence among Friends, and a century-long tradition of "quietism" which emphasized internal discipline and the "machinery of isolation" from worldly temptations. John Bright bridged some of the divides as an unquiet Quaker from a quietist background (literally unquiet because he was one of the most powerful orators of his day). He had no doubt that his Quakerism connected seamlessly to his political liberalism, which took the form of efforts to expand the elective franchise, limit the influence of the landed aristocracy, promote free international trade, disestablish the Church of Ireland, and break up monopolistic

33

power. His approach reached back to the original Quakers, who had resisted paying tithes to support the established church and faced prison for their resistance in the late seventeenth century. A century and a half later, Bright's father continued the resistance to paying church taxes and had suffered substantial losses of seized property. John Bright himself took on the same issue in his first foray into political protest. For the next half-century, he understood politics as an arena for speaking truth and bearing witness.

Bright did not always see eye to eye with the Quaker establishment. He shared anti-slavery convictions, but he prioritized free trade in his own work to the discomfort of some wealthier Friends. At the same time, he thought many Friends were overly cautious in opposing capital punishment, which he deeply deplored. He also feared that the rigid enforcement of acceptable behavior was undermining the future of the Society, writing that the principles that guided Friends were fine but that there were grievous errors in organization and governance. In a lament that sounds quite modern, he complained in 1852 that England's monthly meetings were dying out, with few members to welcome newcomers and children leaving as adults.

In a nation with often bellicose leaders, Bright consistently opposed war and military interventions at personal and political cost, although he steered clear of absolute pacifism and did not join the Peace Society like many other Quakers. He was outspoken in opposition to the Crimean War of 1854–55, telling Parliament that "the angel of death has been abroad throughout the land. You can almost hear the beating of his wings." The conservative press lambasted him, and he lost his seat representing Manchester as a result, although quickly returned instead from the more liberal Birmingham. He worked tirelessly to prevent Britain from recognizing the independence of the South in the United States Civil War—a cause that united his hatred of slavery, his desire to support a democratic nation, and his abhorrence of war. He entered the Cabinet in each of William Gladstone's terms as Prime Minister, but twice resigned to protest a bellicose confrontation with Russia in 1870 and the bombardment of Alexandria, Egypt, in 1882. The second time he moved firmly from insider to outsider: "I have endeavoured to teach ... that the moral law is intended not for individual life only, but for the life and practice of States in their dealing with one another," he told Parliament. "I think that in the present case there has been a manifest violation both of International law and of the moral law, and therefore it is impossible for me to give my support to it."

Bright's career introduces the two themes of this chapter, where we look at Friends who have attained high political office—as cabinet members in parliamentary systems and as Presidents in the United States.

The first question or theme is how Quakerism influenced their approach to politics. What kind of Quakers were they? How important was Quakerism in their daily lives? How, if at all, did Quakerism affect the way that they conducted themselves in seeking and holding office?

The second is the centrality of questions of war and peace. We recognize that we are all fettered by the unspoken norms of our times (John Bright thought that most men should get to vote but not women). Both the assumptions and the specific issues that moved Bright in the nineteenth century, Herbert Hoover in the twentieth century, and Nozizwe Madlala-Routledge in the twenty-first century are distinct to their eras. Nevertheless, we find a common thread, if sometimes thin and frayed, that runs through the careers of many political Friends: attention to disarmament, international reconciliation, and peacebuilding.

The Great War of 1914–18 forced Quakers to make individual and corporate choices that profoundly shaped the Society of Friends. Younger British Friends, including future politician and Nobel Peace Prize winner Philip Noel-Baker, organized the Friends Ambulance Unit to assist medical staff on the Western Front. American Quaker businessman Herbert Hoover organized food relief for residents of occupied Belgium, using Quaker patience to allay German suspicions that he was an Allied spy, and vice-versa. Leading Quakers organized the American Friends Service Committee, originally to provide an alternative to military service for Quaker conscientious objectors.

When the United States entered World War I, President Woodrow Wilson appointed Hoover to head the US Food Administration, which transitioned into the American Relief Administration in 1919. The challenge was not only to feed populations devastated by the wartime Allied food blockade but also to reconstruct canals and railroads in Germany and Central Europe and fight a typhus epidemic. He asked AFSC to distribute relief in Germany because it was apolitical and could earn trust from both the Americans and Germans. AFSC continued to depend on Hoover's goodwill and support for work in Russia 1921–22, and it acceded without much hesitation to his strong suggestion to distance itself from leftwing politics.

For roughly twenty years, from the onset of relief work in Belgium through his work as Secretary of Commerce from 1921–28 to his landslide election to a term as President from 1929 to 1933, Herbert Hoover was one of the world's most widely known Quakers. He was also a very distinctly American variety, raised in close-knit communities of evangelical Friends in West Branch, Iowa and Newberg, Oregon. His membership remained in Oregon with Friends churches in Salem and later Newberg as he attended Stanford University, pursued a very successful globe-spanning career as a mining engineer and entrepreneur, moved in the highest circles in Washington, and retired to Palo Alto, California. Toward the end of the 1920s, the American Friends Service Committee, which was still very closely connected to weighty established Friends, instigated a new Friends Meeting of Washington as a home for the Hoovers that was independent of the Hicksite/Orthodox division among American Quakers. The pastor was a Stanford faculty member on leave from the university at Hoover's request.

Hoover was a self-made man who found a comfortable niche in his country's economic establishment, although he was more willing to try government intervention as the Great Depression worsened in 1931 and 1932 than often credited. His conservatism and standing made him the favorite of Quakers in all parts of the country during the Presidential election of 1928. All the major Quaker periodicals advocated his election, and the prominent author, teacher and minister Rufus Jones kept in direct touch with his campaign. These men saw his candidacy as a vehicle to gain the Society of Friends full acceptance as a mainstream religious group rather than a weird sect of funny-talking eccentrics. Hoover certainly fit right in with the successful Quaker farmers in Midwest and Western states among whom he had grown up and with Quaker businessmen and university faculty of Northeast, delivering the Haverford College commencement speech in 1941.

As President, Hoover pursued a policy of peacebuilding and disarmament that was a practical expression of the peace testimony. In the months between his election and inauguration, he toured Latin America proclaiming a "Good Neighbor" policy; the United States would stop military inventions and build better economic ties. He worked to extend the limits on naval expansion agreed to by the major powers at the Washington Naval Conference of 1921, achieving partial success with the London Naval Treaty of 1930.

Herbert Hoover was a President who happened to be Quaker, not a "Quaker President" whose faith was a primary motivating force. His Quakerism seems to have been deep background and Sunday routine rather than a set of animating principles, and Hoover himself commented that he was a Quaker who didn't work very hard at it. In this light, it is useful to contextualize

Hoover's career with a brief look at how other Quakers responded to the crisis of war and the challenges of peace in the 1910s and 1920s.

Emily Greene Balch was a peace activist before she was a Quaker. She worked with Jane Addams in the Women's Peace Party from 1915. Her strong opposition to American military conscription and sedition laws prompted Wellesley College to fire her from her position as professor of political economy. She helped to organize and then staffed the Women's International League for Peace and Freedom in 1919, which located in Geneva to work with the new League of Nations; she served as an officer or president until 1961. She joined the Society of Friends in 1921 as a very welcome Quaker by convincement and received the Nobel Peace Prize in 1946 for her work with WILPF.

Japanese scholar and diplomat Nitobe Inazō joined the Society of Friends in his twenties while studying at Johns Hopkins University. On returning to Japan after further study in Germany, he served briefly in the Japanese colonial administration in Taiwan and then in several university positions where he emphasized the developmental aspects of colonialism—perhaps the only practical route for a pacifist in a nation that was vigorously expanding its empire. In 1920 he became an under-secretary general of the new League of Nations, supervising the predecessor of UNESCO and helping to resolve a boundary dispute between Sweden and Finland.

Most painful to revisit is the career of A. Mitchell Palmer, a Pennsylvania Quaker from a Hicksite family tradition whose ambitions overcame his conscience as he nearly secured the Democratic Party nomination for President in 1920. If Herbert Hoover was a Quaker by convention and habit, Palmer was Quaker when it was convenient. After being a big man on campus at Swarthmore College, he rose rapidly in Pennsylvania politics, backed Woodrow Wilson's Presidency candidacy, and was offered the position of Secretary of War in 1913. He turned down the offer with an appeal to Quakerism that his biographer suggests was a ploy to hide his disappointment at not being offered the more important position of Attorney General.

> I am a Quaker. As a Quaker War secretary, I should consider myself a living illustration of a horrible incongruity.... In case our country should come to armed conflict with any other, I would go as far as any man in her defense; but cannot, without violating every tradition of my people and going against every instinct of my nature, planted there by heredity, environment, and training, sit down in cold blood in an executive position and use such talents as I possess in the work for preparing such a conflict.[7]

Thereafter he trimmed his sails to political winds. He was adamantly against American involvement in the European war until April 1917, when he was gung-ho for victory. Becoming Attorney General, the chief federal law enforcement official, he staged the notorious Palmer Raids that detained hundreds of suspected Communists and anarchists and fanned what historians call the Red Scare of 1919. At the Democratic Party convention in 1920 he hung a banner proclaiming himself The Fighting Quaker (turned by opponents into The Quaking Fighter for his fear of Bolsheviks). Organized labor despised him and blocked the ambitions of this Quaker by convenience.

Forty years after Herbert Hoover reached the Presidency, another Quaker did the same. Richard Nixon had been a combative and ambitious Congressman and Senator from California and then Vice-President for Dwight Eisenhower from 1953-61. He lost a close election to John F. Kennedy in 1961, lost a race for Governor of California in 1962, and made a surprising comeback to win the Presidency in 1968 and 1972 before resigning in 1974 because of the Watergate scandal. His reputation is deeply damaged by that scandal, his political vindictiveness, and by his conduct of the war in Vietnam, but there are positives as well. His first administration saw the enactment of a broad range of environmental protection measures that retrospectively reflect the Quaker value of stewardship. His opening to China was a move in big power politics, but it also made the world substantially safer. Most Friends applauded the end of military conscription for easing the burden on individual consciences. Most important, negotiation of the first Strategic Arms Limitation Treaty or SALT I with the Soviet Union began a set of steps that have gradually reduced the tensions of the Cold War balance of terror.

This quick review takes us to interlocking questions about Nixon and Quakerism that some readers in the United States may have been anticipating with curiosity and trepidation. Was he a "real Quaker"? If so, what kind of Quaker was that? Were his public statements about Quakerism sincere or a sham— his "first cover-up" in the judgment of historian Larry Ingle? Addressing these questions highlights the way that the Society of Friends in the United States changed and diverged between the 1920s and the 1970s. The change can be encapsulated in a simple comparison. In 1930, Friends Meeting of Washington was a comfortable and compatible place for Herbert Hoover to worship. If Richard Nixon had attended in 1970 (he didn't) he would have seen anti-war literature in the foyer and likely have heard fervent messages denouncing his administration's Vietnam policy.

Nixon was a lifelong member of the Society of Friends. He grew up in East Whittier Friends Church in a town near Los Angeles that had been founded by Quakers. His family's Quaker roots were in Indiana; his second cousin Jessamyn West modeled the Birdwells in her novel *The Friendly Persuasion* on the Milhous family of Nixon's direct ancestors. East Whitter Friends Church was an evangelical congregation that placed less emphasis on distinctive Quaker practices and testimonies than many eastern

Meetings. Within the Society of Friends, it was a very *California* institution at a theological as well as physical distance from London and Philadelphia. Well into Nixon's Presidency when anti-war Quakers called for East Whittier Friends Church to disown him, its pastor turned aside the suggestion with a polite MYOB and a pained sigh.

Nixon publicly claimed Quakerism. He referred repeatedly to his "Quaker heritage from my mother," Hannah Milhous Nixon. He referenced Quaker values like simplicity and silence in speeches and sometimes used Quaker reticence or privacy as a tool to deflect questioners. His common definition of Quakerism was "peace at the center," a concept that he did not elaborate, leaving us to wonder if it meant reliance on the Inner Light or simply introverted stubbornness. Long after the end of his political career, he told a biographer that "the impact of my Quaker heritage on my personality has been underestimated," although he did not elaborate. At the same time, he had little public association with Friends once launched into politics. He once visited Friends Meeting of Washington for a mid-week forum in his early years at Washington. His daughters attended Quaker Sidwell Friends School while he was Vice-President, but the family attended a Congregational and Methodist churches. Once President, he held private worship services in the White House, sometimes led by evangelical Friends. He made an alliance with Billy Graham, the powerful Baptist evangelist who was the most prominent American Christian of his era, and Graham even presided at the memorial service for Hannah Nixon.

Moreover, many Quakers claimed Nixon as one of their own in much the way they had claimed Hoover. Hoover himself mentored Nixon in his early years in Congress. Pastoral Friends in the Midwest and evangelical Friends in the West provided wide support for his career. The fact that he joined the Navy during World War II rather than applying for CO status was no obstacle, since most Quaker men of his age also served in uniform in some capacity—up to 90 percent in Indiana according to historian Tom Hamm and his co-researchers and roughly two-thirds in the Pacific Northwest. The most prominent Quaker Nixonite was D. Elton Trueblood, a widely read theologian and interpreter of Christian beliefs who was also a friend of Hoover. Trueblood advocated for Nixon on the pages of *Quaker Life*, published by Friends United Meeting, and delivered an enthusiastic endorsement of the President at the 1972 Republican nominating convention.

Many Friends, of course, were appalled by Trueblood's convention speech. Quakers who vehemently rejected Nixon came mostly from meetings in university towns, big cities, and the Northeast more generally. Theirs were unprogrammed meetings that increasingly attracted knowledge workers and members of the helping professions such as social work rather than businesspeople and buttoned-down professionals. The civil rights movement, Black rebellion, and Nixon's escalations of the war in Vietnam pushed these meetings toward the opposition politics exemplified by the radicalization of the American Friends Service Committee. There was a simultaneous shift toward universalism and a tendency to define Quakerism by social testimonies while downplaying or even rejecting biblical Christianity. Many such Friends saw little of their social vision in Nixon, and the President reciprocated by scorning what he called "New Quakers." In short, Richard Nixon became a wedge dividing Friends General Conference Quakers from those in Friends United Meeting and what is now Evangelical Friends Church International. The Hoover-Quaker consensus of the 1920s simply could not survive a half century of economic and social change and global crisis.

It is refreshing to end with two recent figures for whom Quakerism has been powerful and formative for personal lives and political careers. Marian Hobbs of Aotearoa/New Zealand

and Nozizwe Madlala-Routledge from South Africa both came to Quakers and to electoral politics from radical activism. As convinced Friends, they found themselves in national cabinets with responsibilities indirectly or directly influencing national military policy and actions that allowed them to emphasize peace building over traditional military roles.

Marian Hobbs was raised in a strongly Roman Catholic family in Christchurch. In her early thirties she became deeply involved in bitterly divisive anti-apartheid activism triggered by the 1981 visit of the all-white South African rugby team to Aotearoa/New Zealand, where it would ironically play the country's beloved All Blacks; named for their uniforms, the All Blacks had included Maori players since the late 1960s. Feeling the need for a new spiritual home in her mid-thirties, she tried the Christchurch Meeting. To her surprise, there were some of the activists with whom she'd worked without knowing they were Quakers. The Meeting became a central part of her life until she entered politics and moved to Wellington. She has retained her identity as a Quaker while being less active in Wellington and then Dunedin where she has lived most recently (and reentered politics on the Otago Regional Council).

Hobbs served twelve years in Parliament from 1996 to 2008. In the early 2000s she was simultaneously Minister for the Environment, Minister for Disarmament and Arms Control, and Associate Minister of Foreign Affairs and Trade for Official Development Assistance. She saw these as overlapping and complementary responsibilities, which included NZAID, the nation's international aid and development agency. On her watch it developed a policy on Preventing Conflict and Building Peace, which includes the statement that "NZAID ensures that all strategies and programmes consider the risks of conflict and are designed to prevent conflict and build peace.... NZAID's programmes follow the principle 'first do no harm' and seek ways to provide positive support to peace processes."

In those roles she was able to redirect the military/policing role. When Australia and New Zealand responded to a request by the government of the Solomon Islands with a Regional Assistance Mission Solomon Islands (RAMSI) to short circuit potential civil war, she used her position to supplement the military and policing intervention to include proactive peace building. "We helped stop the violence," she told a conference on peacemaking in the Pacific, "now we have to help build the peace."[8] She elaborated in a presentation to the Friends World Committee on Consultation Triennial in 2004:

If we eliminate illiteracy and the diseases caused by poor housing and dirty water, then we are peace building. We are eliminating some of the causes of violence. And that's how I answer some of the talkback hosts who question the value of $14-million spent on education in the Solomon Islands. Removing illiteracy there heightens the chances of the people of the Solomon Islands being able to develop their own resources and being able to develop better mechanisms for resolving conflict than an imported AK-47. Yes, that is $14-million not being spent on increasing student allowances or reducing the cost of pharmaceuticals in New Zealand, but it is about peace building.[9]

Nozizwe Madlala-Routledge was deeply committed to anti-Apartheid struggle in South Africa. In 1983 she helped establish the Natal Organization of Women as part of the United Democratic Front, to resist a new constitution that excluded black Africans. One goal was to direct young people toward peaceful protests and vigils rather than violence. Vigils included members of the small community of Durban Quakers, including her future husband, Jeremy Routledge. She tried Meeting because of these pacifist connections when in her mid-thirties and found herself much at home (when she fell asleep

44

during her first time in meeting, she was reassured when one Friend told her that was quite in order). Jeremy was detained for a month under the national state of emergency, and in 1987 she was detained under the Internal Security Act (a law that permitted political activists to be held incommunicado for an indefinite period, without trial), for just under a year. They married in 1989 in a blended African tradition, Christian, and Quaker ceremony. As she became more involved with Quakers, she began to question armed struggle as one of the pillars of the ANC effort. Delivering the Quaker Socialist Society Ada Salter Lecture during Britain Yearly Meeting in 2021, she said: "Today, as a Quaker, I support the peace testimony in full as I look at the aftermath of Apartheid and colonial violence in South Africa. The deep-seated conflict is proving difficult to uproot, confirming the adage that violence breeds violence."[10]

Her journey from activism into politics started when she was asked to help revitalize the South African Communist Party and rebuild its structure after the end of Apartheid. The African National Congress and a cluster of NGOs put her high on the ANC list for Parliament, and she entered Parliament in 1994 in what she describes as an exciting new era. She had to learn fast how to be an MP, but also helped to shape rules of Parliament. She was especially committed to women's issues and women's emancipation, chairing the Parliamentary Women's Group, a multi-Party women's Caucus.

Appointment as Deputy Minister of Defense 1999–2004 was a total surprise. She had 30 minutes to say yes or no when the offer was made—what the *Christian Science Monitor* called either a stroke of brilliance or a monumental blunder. South African Quakers had been pleased when she entered the National Assembly with a feminist agenda. They were conflicted when she accepted appointment as Deputy Defense Minister, with some of them feeling that such direct involvement with the military was simply unQuakerly. After initial pushback, however, her yearly meeting engaged with the concern and developed a Statement on Peace in Africa that can be found in *Living Adventurously*, Central and Southern Africa Yearly Meeting's Faith and Practice. It recognizes that South Africa's "enemies" were poverty and ill health, not foreign adversaries. She values the discernment process that helped her develop a statement defining a peace agenda that is based on social and economic justice.

Under the new government and constitution, defense policy was beginning to evolve from a single focus on military security toward human security, a broader concept of reducing want and fear. Madlala-Routledge took on her position at Defense as a challenge, wanting to help the military in a way that made them want to change. Madlala-Routledge specifically worked to bring more women into national security decisions, continuing her concern to raise up women's voices in South Africa. She helped to form the African Women's Peace Table—a platform bringing together women peace activists and women in the military to look at peace through a gender lens. Many in the military were happy to be asked to do relief work in Mozambique and peacekeeping in Congo and Burundi, with a shift from policing to reconstruction and "developmental peacekeeping." She even floated the idea of renaming the Defense Ministry the Ministry of Peace, and at least one higher up liked the idea. As she has put it, she wanted to free men in the military "to be human."

Her last years in the cabinet were more troubled. She served as Deputy Minister of Health from 2004 to 2007. Her advocacy of science-based responses to the HIV-AIDS crisis clashed with her superior's refusal to allow the use of anti-retroviral therapy and advocacy of untested alternative remedies, such as beetroot, olive oil, African potato and garlic. The President dismissed her from the cabinet ostensibly because of violation of travel policy, but the underlying reason was clear. She was Deputy Speaker of the National Assembly in 2008 before stepping down from elective politics the following year. In 2021 Madlala-Routledge became director of Quaker United Nations Office in Geneva, whose work we touch on in the next chapter.

Madlala-Routledge's new job is the result of new developments among Friends in the twentieth century. The earliest Friends were usually outsiders and often found themselves petitioning the King or Parliament for protection from persecution. Yet, since the days of William Penn, individual Quakers have stepped forward to pro-actively shape their national governments. At times this immersion in electoral politics has been a direct extension of faith as in Emily Green Balch's passion for building a more peaceful world. In the twentieth century, Quakers took steps to magnify their influence by creating organizations grounded in their belief in the possibility of a more just and peaceful world. Such organizations have raised funds, coordinated lobbying efforts, and brought a distinctive presence into all their work, often pointing to their centuries of experience in posing a new way for people to engage their adversaries with love.

Chapter 5

Building Institutional Influence in the Twentieth and Twenty-First Centuries

In 1947, Henry Cadbury of the American Friends Service Committee and Margaret Backhouse representing Friends Service Council of London Yearly Meeting traveled to Stockholm to receive the Nobel Peace Prize on behalf of the Friends worldwide. The award recognized wartime and postwar relief work in areas devasted by World War II and, more generally, the heritage of social service that stretched to similar relief work during and after World War I. The Peace Prize was a recognition worth remembering and celebrating. It also suggests distinctions about the ways in which Quakers have tried to influence civic life. There are important differences among influencing by example, lobbying at a distance, and direct personal interaction with elected officials, diplomats, and other government decision makers.

British Friends would continue to do good and lead by example with help of the Friends Service Council, then Quaker Peace & Service, and since 2001, Quaker Peace and Social Witness, a program of Britain Yearly Meeting. It is the sort of work that Margaret Backhouse summarized in 1947: "Love is very infectious and if Quakers have started the infection they will rejoice." QPSW advocates on behalf of British Friends on peace and peacebuilding, social justice, and environmental sustainability, works in conjunction with like-minded organizations, and supports the work of Friends at the meeting level. Work outside Britain has centered on peacebuilding in Palestine-Israel and East Africa, where it works with Quaker Peace Network-Africa.

Another role undertaken by several Quakers, including

the British Friend Adam Curle, often working with formal organizational support from Friends House London or the AFSC, is as international mediators amid active conflict. This role has sometimes involved Quakers meeting with armed groups usually identified as terrorists, for example, in Nagaland (India), South Africa and Northern Ireland. Curle was called to go to Nigeria during the 1967–1970 Nigerian Civil War as someone who was known to and respected by both sides. In this case, the violence was over before he needed to intervene, but much further action was needed for the work of reconciliation. In reflection he emphasizes the necessity of listening and avoiding judgment yet speaking truth and building relationships of trust over time, as well as the need for transparency in dealing with individuals on different sides of a conflict.

Quaker Peace Network-Africa

In 1998 the Quaker United Nations Office, Friends Committee on National Legislation, and Quaker Peace and Social Witness came together in England with others involved in international peace work for a Quaker Consultation for the Peaceful Prevention of Violent Conflict. It was decided to take the ideas forward in Africa, as there were more wars in Africa than any other continent. However, a second meeting with a focus on Africa was held two years later at the Quaker United Nations Office (QUNO) in New York and at the FCNL office in Washington DC. Participants from Burundi, South Africa, and the Democratic Republic of the Congo met again in Burundi (2002) and Kenya (2004).

QPN-Africa consisted of representatives from Friends peace centers and developmental and educational institutions in Burundi, Kenya, Rwanda, South Africa,

Tanzania, and Uganda. It has had a focus on supporting one another, developing Alternatives to Violence projects and monitoring elections. Burundian Quakers were involved with election observing for the 2005 Burundian elections, and international observers were brought from Rwanda, Democratic Republic of the Congo, Kenya, and overseas. QPN-Africa can serve as a channel of communication between grassroots work and the policy level, and also as a shared "memory" of the many different experiences, and joint learning, across the network, so that these are not lost. It is interested in developing non-formal diplomatic activity in Africa and connecting with the African Union, with help and guidance from QUNO.

AFSC, which had done such important relief work after World War I, began to augment overseas work with domestic social action in the 1930s. In 1942, it worked to help four thousand Japanese Americans to avoid unjust wartime incarceration, often assisting them to secure release and reestablish their lives. It has continued overseas relief and medical assistance in Palestine, Korea during the Korean War, Algeria, Vietnam, and again in North Korea during the 1997 famine as well as other troubled nations like South Sudan. A set of regional offices focused efforts on issues such as Indigenous Nations fishing rights in the Pacific Northwest. The regional office there produced the book *Uncommon Controversy* (1980) which helped to sway public opinion. AFSC also played a supportive role in the 1974 case *United States v. Washington*, which reaffirmed treaty rights. Local offices and programs in across the United States emphasize education, outreach, and advocacy around immigrant rights and racial justice.

Members of AFSC's governing board are Quaker, but

it is independent of any yearly meeting. It has grown increasingly professional, employing many non-Quakers with administrative and organizing skills and with personal connections to disadvantaged communities and communities of color. Unlike its early decades when AFSC was oriented to providing opportunities for individual Friends to be of service, it evolved into a social reform organization oriented to transformative action. In the 1960s and 1970s those changes were especially controversial when many staff saw themselves as radical social activists rather than specifically Quakers doing social action—supporting armed resistance to Apartheid, for example. Echoes of those controversies continue to reverberate, with some Friends no longer seeing AFSC as their "Quaker" organization. However, the change also aligns it more closely with the nineteenth century when Quaker ideals and activism leavened wider reform movements.

AFSC is a prominent part of what we can call Quaker pressure group advocacy or lobbying at a distance. Many Friends are assiduous in contacting their elected officials about pressing issues. Newsletters and announcement time on Sunday can be peppered with requests to pick up your phone, grab your pen, or power up your computer to make a Quaker voice heard. Meetings and churches adopt and publicize minutes and statements of opposition or support for government actions. With thousands of supporters and contributors on its electronic rolodex, AFSC can mobilize hefty citizen advocacy around key issues. In 1980, it was an important part of the Nuclear Freeze Campaign and in 2009 was instrumental in the effort to raise the federal minimum wage. In 2015 its "Governing under the Influence" project mobilized more than a thousand volunteers to ask candidates pointed questions about their stands on specific peace and social justice issues. As we were writing these paragraphs in September 2021, its weekly e-blast asked us to "Tell Congress: Repeal war authorizations and end ongoing military actions around the world!" to add our voice to those mobilized by other organizations arguing pro and con on the same issues.

In 1955, AFSC responded to the Cold War by publishing *Speak Truth to Power: A Quaker Search for an Alternative to Violence.* According to Google Ngrams, the phase "speak truth to power" first appeared in 1915 but was very little used. The AFSC publication seeded a slow but steady increase in popularity as it spread beyond Quaker circles, followed by an explosive upturn in the 1990s—an example of the Quaker message reaching the world in diverse ways.

Some limitations in the structure of AFSC and the need for a more direct presence in Washington led to creation of Friends Committee on National Legislation, which has grown into the most prominent and influential Quaker organization directly engaged with United States national politics. Founded in 1943 in support of rights for conscientious objectors and the Quaker peace testimony, it has offices on Capitol Hill and is the largest religious lobby in Washington. It is the primary organization through which Friends in the United States work on a wide variety of peace and social change issues at the national level. Impetus came from AFSC, whose leaders saw the need for an explicitly political organization to influence the shape of a postwar world that would not be constrained by AFSC's non-profit tax status.[11] The organizing meeting was in Richmond, Indiana to make it clear that it would represent both Eastern and Midwestern Friends (FGC and FUM Friends in twenty-first-century parlance). The first executive secretary, E. Raymond Wilson, came from AFSC staff.

FCNL works directly on the level of the United States Congress. The founding goal in 1943 was to push the United States government toward disarmament, long-term reduction of military spending, and international reconciliation policies. The original commitment to peaceful resolution of international conflicts is now coupled with efforts to promote domestic policies around economic justice, human rights, environmental sustainability, and the needs of Native Americans. It works to directly influence lawmaking and executive branch policy implementation. It has played a critical role in the passage of the Civil Rights Act, the Elie Wiesel Genocide Prevention Act, the Nuclear Non-Proliferation Treaty, and in establishing the Peace Corps.

Its full-time professional staff work directly with Congressional committee staff and with Senators and Representatives to build relationships and push Quaker policy positions, work that may take years to show results. For example, it works as part of a coalition led by Native American organizations that was instrumental in 2021 in the passage of laws directed at fighting the very high levels of violence against Indigenous women. Many years of patient work toward the repeal of the 2001 and 2002 Authorization of Use of Military Force resolutions finally paid off in 2021 with repeal by bipartisan majority in the House of Representatives, although not yet by the Senate.

FCNL Advocacy Teams coordinate thousands of individual lobbyists around the country More than a hundred Advocacy Teams take the FCNL priorities to the home district offices of Senators and Representatives, reinforcing the work of its full-time staff. FCNL supporters also participate in similar state-level groups that focus on issues before their state legislatures. They include Quaker Voice in Washington state, Friends Committee on Legislation of California, Friends Committee on Maine Public Policy, Indiana Friends Committee on Legislation, and Friends Committee on North Carolina Legislation.

There is an informal synergy between FCNL and AFSC. The local programs and offices of AFSC often connect directly with communities impacted by issues such as immigration law, poverty, and racist policing. They mobilize energy and bring a passionate and prophetic voice to public debate. FCNL focuses on the practicalities of moving that prophetic agenda forward in Congress a step at a time without losing sight of its larger goals. It also must take the long view. The passage of the Elie Wiesel Genocide and Atrocity Prevention Act in 2019 culminated a decade of work that began by convening a multi-organization working group in 2009, drafting legislative language in multiple versions in 2013, 2015, and 2016, securing an Executive Order in 2015, and finally bipartisan sponsorship of successful legislation. As Paul told the early Christians in Corinth, "Love is patient ... always hopes, always perseveres."

Unlike groups that use their Washington presence to hammer relentlessly for a narrow agenda, FCNL strives to develop and maintain a reputation for bridge-building and for seeking to help members from both sides of the aisle find common ground. Openness and transparency about goals is essential to its work. When a staff member shows up to talk with a Senator about foreign policy, she knows in advance that she will be urged to find non-military solutions to problems and can enter a conversation with no hidden agendas, even if immediate agreement is unlikely. FCNL's main office, one block from the Hart Senate Office Building, provides a neutral and private venue where members of Congress and staff can meet to explore common ground without political posturing.

This same role is one of the important functions of the Quaker United Nations Office (QUNO), which operates in both New York and Geneva. Quaker Houses in both cities are venues for the quiet diplomacy of face-to-face conversations and informal forums where representatives to the UN and its agencies can interact without their briefing books and talking points. Individuals who would not meet in fully public settings—or at least not meet productively—will accept QUNO invitations. Many of these meetings, of course, are off the record with varying degrees of confidentiality and depend on the discretion of QUNO staff, whether they involve two people sitting over coffee or dinners for twenty individuals. QUNO Geneva may also host gatherings in other cities around the world when they are the sites of important meetings. Since 2013, it has arranged twenty off-the-record meetings for diplomats to help build trust and ambition in the UN climate negotiations and regularly speaks at meetings of the Intergovernmental Panel on Climate Change, where it is the only faith-based observer organization. One of the tasks and skills of QUNO staff is to listen carefully to discern who best to invite to such meetings. Confidential meetings "give people a space to listen," in Jonathan Woolley's words. QUNO gatherings are "a space to connect and test ideas" without being held to specific positions and "a safe space mentally and physically for people to share."

The New York Quaker House on East 48th Street is close enough to the UN to be convenient but distant enough to be inconspicuous. In 2003, Jack Patterson and Lori Heninger described QUNO as lubricant to facilitate interactions, so they do not become overheated. Lunchtime meetings where diplomats balance plates on their knees in a living room are much different from a formal luncheon with place cards; it is understood that conversations can be frank because no minutes are circulated. The meetings have often been designed to help find common ground for upcoming issues. Quaker House early on was a venue where South African diplomats could meet representations from other African countries, and where diplomats quietly discussed finding a new Secretary-General after the death of Dag Hammarskjold. The ambassador from Malta first raised the idea for a Law of the Sea Treaty at a QUNO dinner for representatives from Mediterranean countries. At a luncheon preceding the Third Special Session on Disarmament in 1988, the representatives of Italy and Colombia stood up and announced that they would collaborate to launch a United Nations registry on the international trade in conventional weapons — which is now functioning. Quaker House can also be the site for very private one-on-one meetings.

A more elaborate variation was to invite diplomats and their families to come together for a few days in the Catskill Mountains ninety miles from New York. The site is Mohonk Mountain House, a resort founded by Quakers that had hosted a Conference on International Arbitration from 1885 to 1916 and was a favorite of affluent Quaker families from the New York area. Before smart phones, it was also far enough from the UN that attendees could not constantly check in with their office. According to Stephen Collett, writing in 2007, the meetings gained a strong reputation.

> The "Mohonk" meeting has become a familiar term around UN Headquarters. The Quaker Office is regularly approached by diplomats and UN Secretariat officials with suggestions of topics and participants which they feel might benefit from a "Mohonk/ ... And there have been a number of cases when the results were specific enough to be referred to around the UN as the "Mohonk solution" ... QUNO filled a similar role in helping UN delegates and Secretariat to prepare for the 1995 Fourth World Conference on Women held in Beijing. There was a time close to the Women's Conference when the final chapter of the Beijing agreement—the chapter on implementation measures—was referred to within the inner circle of diplomats negotiating these documents as the "Mohonk chapter."[12]

QUNO is successor to an earlier Friends presence in Geneva established to work with the League of Nations. After World War II, Friends sought the same relationship with the United Nations. The UN approved consultative status for Friends World Committee for Consultation in 1948. Because the UN requires non-governmental organizations that want to be represented be international rather than national in scope, FWCC provides the umbrella for QUNO. Its New York office is funded by and jointly administered with the American Friends Service Committee and is formally a part of AFSC. The Geneva office is legally a Swiss charity that is administered jointly by FWCC and Britain Yearly Meeting, which has long provided very substantial financial support. The UN granted QUNO "general consultative status" on 2002, allowing staff to participate in committee meetings and to suggest agenda items for the UN Economic and Social Council. They can make statements on current issues, respond to consultative documents, and prepare policy proposals. It is also active in the World Trade Organization, the Human Rights Council, the International Labour Organization, and other multilateral organizations. Long-term accomplishments cited by QUNO Geneva include international agreements on child soldiers, landmines, generic medicines, the rights of prisoners, and the right of conscientious objection to military service. On-going work includes the rights of migrants and the close connection between peacebuilding and human rights.

Britain Yearly Meeting appointed Christine Peaker to the new role of Parliamentary Liaison Secretary in the early 1990s. The role was intended both to represent Quaker views to Parliament and Government and to educate Friends and their Meetings about national political debate. The position was initially well-funded with administrative support and operated with some autonomy. Michael Bartlet, who served in the role from 1996 to 2013, points to influence on Quaker concerns of freedom of information, legalization of same-sex marriage in religious premises, and helping to create a "right of discharge" for young people in the armed forces recruitment. He described his work "as a combination of working on centrally discerned Quaker concerns such as 'Peace Tax' and same sex marriage in religious premises; working in secular and religious coalition such as on land mines or combating increasingly harsh attitudes to refugees and asylum seekers; and 'political education' by writing articles and meeting with Friends in their Meetings." Both Peaker and Bartlet regularly attended the political conferences of the several parties. It was for several years possible to arrange an occasional Meeting for Worship through the good offices of the Speaker's Chaplain.

The work of the Parliamentary Liaison Secretary has faced some challenges. There has always been an ambivalence and at times cynicism among British Friends about party political engagement. Bartlet has commented that in the 1990s and early twenty-first century Friends may has preferred direct action and the perceived "purity" of single-issue politics rather than the painstaking compromises necessitated by parliamentary politics. In addition, a significant aspect of the role has been working with Quaker Parliamentarians. However, no Quakers served in the House of Commons between 2005 and 2015.

In 2021, the liaison role was part of the portfolio of the Public Affairs and Media Manager, whose responsibilities spanned social media, interfaith organizing, and a Scottish Parliament officer. Grace Da Costa described her work as divided between directly developing contacts and relationships with members of Parliament, coordinating advocacy with other faith-based and civil society organizations, and encouraging and assisting British Quakers in contacting MPs and working on local issues. Quakers' small numbers and progressive approach can make it difficult to reach many parliamentarians, although Da Costa notes that video conference meetings are easier to arrange than time in person.

Both Britain Yearly Meeting and QUNO also cooperate on key issues with the Quaker Council for European Affairs, a small organization that has been based in Brussels since its founding in 1979. QCEA works to support peaceful conflict resolution and human rights within the context of the European Union and the Council of Europe. It helps coordinate and articulate a voice for the small numbers of Quakers in Europe to influence

European policy. In recent years it has been especially active on the transnational issues of immigration and refugees that affect the entire European Union.

All of the organizations face the challenge of setting priorities. Friends know that every meeting and church has members who are passionate about a wider range of issues than the group can deal with effectively. The situation is no different for national and international organizations. In Britain, the Yearly Meeting and Meeting for Sufferings (the standing representative body entrusted with the general care of matters affecting Britain Yearly Meeting) set directions for Quaker advocacy according to three criteria: Do Quakers have something distinctive to say? Is the issue important to Quakers? Is their advocacy likely to have a positive impact? QUNO's issues arise from the global network of Friends World Committee on Consultation, which raises up the voices and concerns of Friends in Africa, Asia, and Latin America alongside those of other Friends. FCNL sets legislative priorities through a bottom-up process in which hundreds of individual churches and meetings forward ideas to be prioritized by the representative general committee.

The extraordinary story of Sam and Miriam Levering shows the links among several of these organizations as they pursued their indefatigable work to secure a worldwide Law of the Sea treaty. The Leverings were members of North Carolina Yearly Meeting who made their living from an orchard in southwestern Virginia. In 1943 Sam represented his yearly meeting at the Richmond, Indiana gathering that created Friends Committee on National Legislation, and he clerked its executive committee from 1956 to 1972 (which he admitted later might have been a bit too long). Even while working with Miriam to manage his orchard and cope with changing demands for fruit, he was equally active with the Board of Peace and Christian Social Concerns of Five Years Meeting (now Friends United Meeting).

Their lives got even busier in 1972. Philadelphia Quakers offered to finance a year's work in Washington with FCNL to prevent legislation that might undermine efforts to negotiate a comprehensive Law of the Sea treaty. Sam decided to take it on. A late frost that decimated the year's fruit crop and left little to do on the farm made the decision easier. Miriam and Sam shared a small office at FCNL where they rolled out mats to sleep on the floor. The work continued for the next eleven years. They lobbied Congress against proposals for the United States to claim special rights to ocean resources. Allies in the State Department got him appointed to the Public Advisory Committee on the Law of the Sea. Miriam focused on educating the public through an Ocean Education Project which was able to receive funds to allow them to attend the international Law of the Sea Conferences beginning in 1974.

Their work—still from the FCNL base—spiraled. Sam became a key, unofficial advisor to Elliot Richardson, the head of the US delegation. They spent more time in New York, where small groups of delegates hashed out differences around the dining room table at QUNO's Quaker House, where the Leverings stayed when in New York. Because private national organizations could not be part of the Law of the Sea discussion, the Ocean Education Project officially represented Friends Committee on National Legislation. QUNO was again of assistance at the 1975 Conference in Geneva, where Miriam and her United Methodist allies published a newsletter that also marked out common ground. The extraordinary work of Miriam and Sam wound up in 1982 when negotiators hammered out and signed a United Nations Convention of the Law of the Sea. It went into effect in 1994 after the 60th nation ratified it, and164 UN members have now done so.[13]

The inspiring experience of the Leverings encapsulates some of the generalizations that we offer in the next chapter—the importance of a supportive Quaker network for Quaker lobbyists and elected officials, the practical necessity of alliances, the importance of patience and persistence, and the value of a non-antagonistic approach to disagreements.

Chapter 6

Engaging the Powers

True godliness don't turn men out of the world, but enables them
to live better in it, and excites their endeavours to mend it...
Christians should keep the helm and guide the vessel to its port;
not meanly steal out at the stern of the world and leave those that
are in it without a pilot to be driven by the fury of evil times upon
the rock or sand of ruin.
William Penn, 1682

In our final chapter, we explore what it means for contemporary
Friends to keep the helm and endeavor to guide our world to
port. We draw on the experiences of people who are currently
or recently in public office, or who devote full time to working
directly with elected officials and diplomats, in order to offer
suggestions about what it is like to be a Quaker in politics —
both the challenges and contributions. Our sources are the
direct words of Friends, gathered from direct interviews over
Zoom, correspondence, online roundtables, podcast interviews,
webinars, and published talks and essays They include the
following Friends who serve or have served in elective office:
Marian Hobbs, Jo Vallentine, Nozizwe Madlala-Routledge,
Catherine West, Tania Mathias, Alex Cole-Hamilton, Judith
Kirton-Darling, Rush Holt, DeAnne Butterfield, George Gastil,
Kathy Hyzy, Michael Snarr, Jasmine Krotkov, Lon Burman, and
Wendy Gooditis. They also include people who have worked to
organize a political presence for Quakers or have filled formal
roles interacting with national legislatures and the United
Nations: Jonathan Woolley, Jeremy Routledge, Michael Bartlet,
Grace Da Costa, Diane Randall, Jim Cason, Bobby Trice, Diana
Ohlbaum, Lizzy Biddle, Amelia Kagan, and Bridget Moix.[14]

Their positions and roles have included membership in national and multinational parliaments and legislative bodies, American state legislatures, borough and city councils, and school boards.[15] Experienced Friends may recognize similarities between some of the things that make Quakers stand out in the political arena and practices such as the careful discernment of a clearness committee or the nonjudgmental listening of worship sharing.

We recognize that this list tilts toward people from the United States, but we have talked with Friends in several other countries as well. We also regret that we lack a time machine to travel back to talk with important figures like Ada Salter, the adamant socialist reformer and pacifist who was the first woman elected to the council of the Borough of Bermondsey in southeast London and would go on to serve as its mayor; Labour MP Alfred Salter; Paul H. Douglas, both a Quaker and a combat-tested United States Marine who was one of the most liberal members of the United States Senate from 1948 to 1967; or Philip Noel-Baker, long-serving Labour MP whose decades of work for disarmament earned a Nobel Peace Prize in 1958.

We recognize that many Friends have served in prominent roles in democratic governments as diplomats, judges, and influential civil servants. The career of Nitobe Inazō is a prominent example. In Kenya, the Quaker reputation for integrity opened career paths for many. Benjamin Ngaira served as public service commissioner for Jomo Kenyatta, the first president of the independent nation. In 1961, Thomas Lung'aho was on a national commission to survey the Kenyan educational system. Simeon Shitemi, who has also been prominent in FWCC, filled several roles as permanent secretary in the ministries of health, tourism, wildlife and fisheries, as director of the departments of education and foreign trade, and as head of diplomatic delegations. Many other Quakers have served in important appointive positions and in elected office in Kenya and Burundi, and we regret that we are not able to offer a fuller discussion. Their contributions and experiences merit another full book.

We also recognize that we have not addressed the broad arena of nonviolent direct action outside conventional political channels, actions that range from efforts to extend rights within democracies to efforts to overthrow oppressive regimes. Such actions vigorously and sometimes forcibly challenge the consciences of people in power, and they may extend to direct interference with the operations of the state. A notable example is the Freedom Ride organized by Bayard Rustin in 1948 to challenge segregation in the American South, a predecessor to better known Freedom Rides in the 1960s. The freedom riders could have looked back to the New England Friends who in 1841 participated in "ride-ins" to protest segregated railroad coaches. Quakers in South Africa disrupted apartheid with actions along a spectrum from quiet noncompliance to open defiance leading to imprisonment. American Earle Reynolds defied both the United States and the Soviet militaries by sailing his yacht *Phoenix* into nuclear test zones. Less headline-making but very Quakerly has been the Quaker Earth Action Team, who challenged a Philadelphia bank with Quaker roots to live up to its environmental goals with traditional organizing, but also with actions like holding meetings for worship in bank lobbies and singing "Which Side Are You On" to each member of the bank's board of directors at a shareholder meeting. As we noted in Chapter 1, there is an extensive literature on Quaker activism and peacemaking, and we commend that work to our readers' attention as we return our attention to the arena of parliaments and legislatures.

British MP Catherine West addresses a fundamental question when she writes that "alongside other Quaker values such as simplicity and sustainability, actively advancing the cause of equality is both a political imperative and a spiritual vocation." She is addressing a concern that weaves through

Quaker history: Does the hustle and bustle and horse-trading of political life undermine and even contradict a full spiritual life? Should Friends maintain the position of virtuous outsiders who point out the mistakes and sins of others without risking the same sins themselves? We certainly do not argue that politics is for everyone; some of us are far better suited to a contemplative life than one of lobbying, campaigning, and legislative committee rooms. Nevertheless, we agree with her desire to show people who are disillusioned with politics that one of the best responses is to participate as fully as they are able, because "politics is essentially about changing the world around us for the better through dialogue rather than force."[16] Put another way, politics is the recognized process for making decisions that affect an entire community, province, or nation, so being completely uninvolved is not possible.

Individual Friends will continue to argue whether it is better to work within the political process or to apply pressure from the outside. The choice to push from the outside with rallies, vigils, and letters to the press can be especially appealing when one's own elected representatives seem unlikely to agree with Quaker stands, as with the immensely frustrating run-up to the Iraq War. We suggest that what Quakers have to offer from the outside—organize marches, hold up signs—is similar to any other pressure group. What they have to offer as participants within the political process, however, is vital and even distinct— the willingness to listen across the aisle and search unrelentingly for common ground.

Addressing Australian Quakers, Jo Vallentine took the question head on. Many people see politics as a dirty business, she acknowledged, and it is likely "that is why Quakers, among the more critical and perceptive members of society, shy away from direct involvement in electoral politics." She preferred to think of herself as an activist who happened to get elected to Parliament for six years. Nevertheless, despite detailing the constraints and pettiness of day-to-day work in the Australian Senate, she concluded with an endorsement of political involvement: "So, rather than giving up on the institution of Parliament because of its hierarchy, its patriarchy, its distance from the community, my plea is for greater understanding and more involvement, to make the system work better.... It is my hope that Quakers, and others, will not find what I have said about the dilemmas of political life daunting, but rather an encouragement to be bold in whatever way is appropriate, as guided by the light within."[17]

Lobbying raises the same issues as electoral politics. The very words "lobbying" and "lobbyist" summon up distasteful images of self-interested corporations and their hired guns pressuring for special legislative treatment. Lobbying is often considered as amoral. It sometimes is seen as the action of angry people demanding Congress address a particular issue that is not popular with the public or seen as a threat to general well-being. Diana Ohlbaum, a senior strategist at Friends Committee for National Legislation loves "saying that I am a Quaker Peace Lobbyist. This blows people's minds. They seem like three words that don't belong together. Quaker: isn't that a brand of oatmeal? Peace: you mean there's really someone lobbying for peace? Lobbyist: I thought lobbyists were bad. This makes a great start to a discussion, and people really brighten up once they hear the explanation."

Friends with whom we talked have generally found good support from their Quaker communities as they have actively pursued politics. Judith Kirton-Darling, who represented a Northern England constituency in the European Parliament, found strong support from Friends in Europe as well as Britain. The commitments of office, two small children back home, and the 3700-kilometer commute between Perth and Canberra made Jo Vallentine's attendance at meeting for worship irregular, but it was always rewarding: "The strength in the silence is wonderful, the contributions of others usually helpful, and the supportive fellowship of Friends, encouraging."[18] She notes that Canberra Friends, although not her home meeting, were especially supportive because they are familiar with the day-to-day pressures of political life. Lon Burman, who served for eighteen years as a Quaker in the very conservative Texas legislature, found that his involvement with Friends Committee on National Legislation to be a lifeline.

Involvement with Quakers helped Jasmine Krotkov, from Great Falls, Montana, realize that politics can be much more than a necessary evil. She already had some experience in the political realm when visiting Washington to advance the needs of Postmasters. Back home, she encountered two prompts to stand for the state legislature. One was hearing someone else say they were planning to run and thinking "I could do that!" After hearing more than one person say that "we need a Quaker on the judiciary committee," which deals with criminal justice laws, she worked with a clearness committee to discern whether to run. She continued to meet with an anchor or support committee while she was in office to help her avoid the "rock and sand of ruin" (to reference William Penn).

Friends do need to be careful not to use their church or meeting as a venue and forum for pressing elected officials on favorite causes rather than allowing them space to refresh their spiritual lives. Many Quakers are passionate and sometimes single-minded about issues like climate change, nuclear power, policing, Palestine-Israel relations, and racial justice. Some are not shy about expressing and urging their views in meeting for worship. Indeed, we decided that one of the 10 a.m. meetings for worship that we once attended was edging into "meeting for discussing the Sunday *New York Times*." Legislators and MPs are regularly asked to support causes and enlist behind issues, and their Quaker communities can be most helpful by offering spiritual nourishment, not using worship to lecture them about favorite causes and perhaps push them away. One elected representative drew back from their home meeting when it seemed as if their presence might he harming worship as a gravitational attractor that warped ministry toward the hot issue they were facing.

A related point is that Friends in unprogrammed meetings should not assume that every Quaker who enters the political arena is automatically Labour, Green, or progressive left Democrat. It is possible to be a Conservative MP such as Tania Mathias, who combines a personal commitment to peacemaking while supporting market-oriented domestic policies, positions that John Bright and Herbert Hoover would likely have approved. She noted with gratitude that following her election, a respected older Friend rose after meeting to congratulate her and note than many earlier Quakers had also served as Conservatives (the most recent being independent-minded Richard Body who served a total of thirty-nine years in the House of Commons before standing down in 2001).

Evangelical Friends churches in the United States also tend to have a different range of political affiliations and policy preferences, particularly around domestic policy questions, than do unprogrammed Friends. The difference stems in part from social context. Friends in rural Iowa and small-town Oregon are likely to have different interests and concerns than do adamantly liberal Friends in big cities and university towns. Their challenge may be to differentiate themselves from hard-right fundamentalists. Lon Fendall is an evangelical Friend who worked for many years as an aide to US Senator Mark Hatfield. His suggestion in 1996 still holds: "Evangelical Friends choosing to run for elective office today who firmly embraced Quaker convictions about peace and justice would have a hard time in the Republican Party," but also among progressive secular Democrats.[19]

Friends are called to see beyond pure yes/no issue advocacy

as well as partisan politics. Single-track activists need to accept that successful policy making usually requires working within a coalition. After all, Quakers have a clear and persuasive voice but a very small share of the electorate. Sometimes the alliances are straightforward, such as Quakers in the United States working with Mennonites and Church of the Brethren as three historic peace churches, or Quakers in Britain clubbing with Methodists and the Salvation Army to lobby the Labour Party.[20] Alex Cole-Hamilton, a member of the Scottish Parliament and leader of Scotland's Liberal Democrats, recently emphasized the Quaker orientation to resolving conflicts and forging alliances as central to his political approach. Britain Yearly Meeting works with different coalitions on different issues; faith groups involved with refugee policy have been largely Christian while climate justice work has been more broadly interfaith.

Because every political party is an umbrella that shelters a range of interests and subgroups, representatives to state and national legislative bodies are automatically members of internal coalitions. This is especially apparent in parliamentary systems with strong parties and party discipline. A Quaker MP or junior cabinet minister can offer suggestions but must follow party decisions in in most cases. Marian Hobbs recalls that her parliamentary experience required constant and necessary compromise. "There is loyalty to the team and the overall goal of fairness to all, even when you have doubts about the wisdom, rightness of some of the individual decisions. But to make a fuss, to stand alone, might distract from the main goal."[21]

The experience of Jo Vallentine offers an interesting contrast. Australia's system of proportional representation (rather than single member winner-take-all or first-past-the-post districts) put her in the Senate as a member of the tiny Nuclear Disarmament Party, as an Independent when the NDP fragmented, and finally as a Green. She had much more freedom to promote progressive policies, but without the support of a strong party team.[22] She relished the freedom that came with Independent status that allowed her to focus on educating the public about the militarization of Australia by raising questions that challenged and embarrassed both major parties. She was happy to acknowledge her "irritant value" and enjoyed making the major parties uncomfortable and proving that "someone from the community can get into the Senate and have a go."[23]

In the United States, FCNL works hard to build coalitions among both faith-based lobby organizations and secular groups with shared objectives on legislation. Former FCNL General Secretary Diane Randall sees this as both a strategic and a practical choice. FCNL in joining with others can leverage collective power. In doing this, she notes, they also explicitly recognize the variety of religious experience that can make visible the universality of God's love. As the largest and oldest faith-based organization on Capitol Hill, FCNL often provides the staff who can chair coalition committees on a wide range of issues such as the Interfaith Criminal Justice Coalition. The breadth of the issues the organization addresses and its comprehensive vision of creating God's kingdom on earth allows it to better see the inter-linking nature of the concerns carried by many faith-based lobbyists who are most often focused on a smaller set of objectives. Its long-term focus recognizes that while desired provisions in a bill may be removed or reduced, what remains may still warrant support.

At the state level in the United States, Quakers from Annapolis and Patapsco Meetings in the state of Maryland have described how an initial book group reading about unjust incarceration morphed into a statewide Maryland Alliance for Justice Reform (MAJR) that brought major reforms to the Maryland criminal justice system while helping to block regressive legislation. They report that "Members from other Maryland advocacy groups persuaded MAJR to lend its support to existing initiatives that had struggled for traction in past years. Some members of these groups were invited to join MAJR and became members of our executive committee, helping us to make better-informed policy decisions." They also advise that "One important lesson learned from these allies was the recognition that we should not attempt to reinvent the wheel on any policy matter where other advocates already had laid the groundwork and begun a policy campaign."[24]

Building a successful coalition may involve compromises that upset and even appall those Friends who, at worst, are issue absolutists. Quaker decision-making eschews explicit compromise because it is founded on the belief that prayerful waiting on the Spirit will allow everyone to come to the same right choice which often differs from any initial proposal or position. The practice may be a bit less pure. Committee reports to the larger body may sometimes embody compromises — and they are more effective and spirit-led if the compromises are acknowledged rather than left unspoken. Listening to the Spirit in meeting for business may involve quiet assessments of common ground. Continuing revelation may result in slower progress as not all Friends come to a solution at the same time. The ideal, however, is that what emerges is something more than a mere vector-sum of different views.

The idea of compromise can also be difficult because many Quakers get involved with politics because their policy goals have grown out of deep spiritual conviction. Nevertheless, once someone is in office, whether the US Congress or a local council, they cannot remain a single-issue politician (or one trick pony to reference the Paul Simon song). George Gastil, who has served on a southern California school board and a city council comments that it may be better to have a good result with 5-0 vote than a slightly better policy adopted 3 to 2 and leaving a dissatisfied minority. Another Friend approaches problems from multiple perspectives, understanding that there is more than one legitimate point of view. Because there is a larger truth, it is acceptable to change one's mind. Says a British MP, be prepared to be surprised, be prepared to be moved. "Noticing is a huge skill," says DeAnne Butterfield about the need to be open to the ideas and views of others.

Voting for an imperfect policy may not be a failure of integrity, and the work of building cooperative relationships may be more important that a specific policy outcome. Kathy Hyzy is a city council member from a mid-sized Portland, Oregon suburb who also represents all the cities in her large suburban county on a regional transportation policy committee. She is a deeply committed environmentalist and climate activist. The committee faced a transportation proposal that Kathy and climate activists strongly opposed, but that clearly had a committee majority in favor. Should she allow the measure to pass as part of a unanimous "consent agenda" with no individual votes recorded or move it to the regular agenda where everyone would have to vote yea or nay. She decided not to force the issue, hoping to build trust that might allow her to argue other questions more effectively.

Even in the practical world of compromises, concessions, and coalitions, Quakers find that approaching politics from a place of faith opens unexpected doors. Their history can inspire respect even from political opponents, and a powerful and positive reputation can follow them even into local areas. People tend to assume that Quaker officials must be highly principled, even if they may disagree with the positions that are based on those principles. FCNL staff report that talking about their own faith background helps to find common ground with some conservatives about protecting God's environment, and that the history of Quaker work for peace and disarmament can open conversations. Simply articulating a faith perspective as a lobbyist causes Congressional staff to sit up and listen because it is so unlike the usual lobbyist approach. When appropriate, an FCNL staff member may take the opportunity to worship and pray together with congressional staff at the conclusion of a lobby visit or otherwise step outside the realm of the political.

Time and again we heard the word "heart." Bring our hearts to the work of politics, says Jasmine Krotkov, who always reminded other legislators that their work is about people, not laws for their own sake. DeAnne Butterfield, an experienced lobbyist who has served on the Boulder, Colorado City Council, says Friends should talk about what's in their heart when visiting with elected officials and remember that Spirit is in the room with you and those you are trying to persuade. "We are not alone in this work if we pay attention. If we bring our Light, it can illuminate for all." Another Friend comments that "no matter whom we were meeting with or what position they took on a policy issue, our belief in the Divine Spark in every person, in the possibility of transformation for all of us, and in deep listening to seek Truth together guided our approach. That isn't always easy. But it is what has continually drawn me back to FCNL and Quaker organizations, and it is a big part of why I became a Friend."

A younger activist reports that speaking truth to power may result in an unforeseen moment of transformation. She visited the office of newly elected Republican Senator along with sixteen other Quakers. It was early in his term, and they did not know what to expect. With prayer and concentrated openheartedness, the FCNL advocates shared their stories and asked the Senator's military attaché to support the Elie Wiesel Prevention of Genocide and Atrocities Act. "This officer really listened to us and aligned with us and our Quaker beliefs to prevent [future] military involvement."

Quaker openness earns a reputation for honest non-partisan interactions. Much of FCNL's work is reaching across differences with respect. They can note when a Republican is looking for support and a Democrat has similar concerns on an issue, and to seize the opportunity to bring them together. At times this means offering them space to meet at the at the FCNL offices to avoid being seen talking to each other in the Capitol corridors. We have seen that the Quaker United Nations Office offers similar opportunities for opposing parties to interact without committee agendas and name cards.

Time and again, we hear the same point: Quakers in politics are a refreshing voice because they try to listen carefully to everyone and look for the merits in what they say, even with people who are on record opposing something of great value to Friends. Jo Vallentine used social settings to seek out opposing Members of Parliament to search for shared interests and was sometimes surprised. For example, she developed a working relationship with a right-of-center Liberal around a concern for human rights. Another Friend noted that colleagues of the opposite party appreciated her evenhandedness as a legislative committee chairperson. Several Friends noted the importance of listening carefully to constituents as well as fellow politicians and looking for common ground with someone who is very unlikely to vote for your position. Catherine West advises everyone to talk to their MP, even if they don't expect them to agree with your "ask" or request. Bring your principles and concerns to bear and open a dialogue—you never know where it might lead. Citizens are advised to bring stories to their meetings with elected officials, not just data and talking points, and we need to remember that politicians have their own stories that we need to listen to.

Politicians are accustomed to being yelled at by angry constituents and harangued by members of other parties. When Friends respectfully disagree while seeking common ground, officials can be taken aback, and a way forward can sometimes open. We might think of the similar role of the clerk in business meeting, where listening carefully to every comment and viewpoint is basic. Officials expecting to be berated will *sometimes* respond positively to careful listening for the seed of Truth in everyone. Younger Friend Bobby Trice says: "I was so refreshed by FCNL's approach to lobbying in the manner of Friends. After years of cynicism, I started seeing that of God in each person, including in the members of Congress with whom I disagreed."

Quaker educator Parker Palmer calls this aspect of the Quaker approach to politics the "habit of humility," which means "accepting the fact that my truth is always partial and may not be true at all—so I need to listen with openness and respect, especially to 'the other,' as much as I need to speak my own voice with clarity and conviction."[25] He speaks elsewhere about the need "to listen to each other openly and without fear, learning how much we have in common despite our differences" and the even more challenging need "to deepen our empathy for the alien 'other' as we enter imaginatively into the experiences of people whose lives are radically unlike our own."[26]

None of this suggests that Friends abandon their commitments to ending armed conflicts, bringing racial justice and greater economic equality, and caring for God's creation. It is perfectly fine to be loud, says Virginia state legislator Wendy Gooditis. She has been willing to march across the aisle to "scold" a colleague after they have spoken but tries to do so with a smile while recognizing that their views are sincerely held. At times it may be useful to "upset the apple cart in a creative way" to call attention to minority positions, as Jo Vallentine sometimes challenged the massive parliamentary rule book. We can articulate these positions clearly and forcefully and expect those with whom we interact to be as respectful of Friends as they try to be with others. Referring to the FCNL "we seek" statements, Rush Holt, who served sixteen years in the U S Congress, says that "it is important to have that standard to repair to."

At the same time, an open and transparent process is important, again as in meeting for business. "Always I was searching for neutral language, for open processes," Marian

Hobbs writes about her service as a New Zealand cabinet minister. "It was the process that was my focus. If the process was trusted, if people's fears [about genetically modified crops] were heard and lessened, then I might be able to lower the conflict." On another issue, she wrote in 2005, "[T]he extremes are vocal, but with time and clear information and meetings of all kinds, we are working to establish clarity and a way forward." Is it so different from a Meeting for Clarity inside the Society of Friends? Peace and resolution at a national level take time, reflection, clear articulation and listening.[27]

Quakers are fond of the phrase "speak truth to power," often citing it as their mission and their way of acting in the public realm. It is a phrase with great resonance that has entered the general vocabulary of progressive activists, and there are times when it is both apt and necessary. However, there is a certain danger in using the phrase too blithely. It suggests that Quakers who have truth are on one side of an equation and that people with power are on the other—that we are the virtuous outsiders speaking to those others who are insiders. We might better think, along with Catherine West, of trying to "reform the practice of power" through our comportment and practices.

We want to close with encouragement. Politics needs Quakers who bring the values of openness, patience, and humility to elected bodies at all levels, along with the practice of regarding political opponents as worthy of respect. It also needs people who have been influenced positively by Quaker values and approaches even if they do not identify as Quaker. When asked what they would say to a young Quaker interested in politics, former MP Tania Mathias says, "Do it!" Former Congressman Rush Holt says "Sure!" and Wendy Gooditis says, "Go for it!" Judith Kirton-Darling sees standing for elected office at any level as a civic responsibility for those with the right temperament and skills because "that side of civic life is really important." Jo Valentine affirms that political office can be "an amazing opportunity for service." Friends can bring to political life a deep concern for issues of peace and justice that they share with other activists, but also a groundedness in the Spirit, the firm foundation that makes it possible to hear everyone's story and bring full and loving attention to everyone's concerns. Marian Hobbs urges the importance of finding even the smallest shared ground and seeking out truth in the middle of conflict. In a nutshell: stay grounded in the Spirit to find common ground without giving ground on our basic convictions and vision of a just world.

References

1. www.quaker.org.uk/documents/an-introduction-to-quaker-peace-social-witness-nov-2018 accessed 8/10/2021
2. Jo Vallentine and Peter D. Jones, *Quakers in Politics: Pragmatism or Principle*. Backhouse Lecture, Religious Society of Friends in Australia. 1990, 5.
3. Esther Mombo and Cecile Nyiramana, *Mending Broken Hearts and Rebuilding Shattered Lives*. 2016 Swarthmore Lecture (London: Quaker Books, 2016), 30.
4. Anna Fritz, "I Hold You Up," from *On a High Hill*, c. 2016, annafritz.com.
5. Quoted in Margaret Hope Bacon, *Mothers of Feminism: The Story of Quaker Women in America* (New York: Harper and Row, 1986), 190.
6. Bacon, *Mothers of Feminism*, 193.
7. Quoted in Stanley Coben, *A. Mitchell Palmer: Politician* (New York: Columbia University Press, 1963), 71.
8. Marian Hobbs, "Securing a Peaceful Pacific: A Conference on Preventing and Resolving Conflict in the Pacific," Oct. 16, 2004. https://www.beehive.govt.nz/speech/%E2%80%9Csecuring-peaceful-pacific-conference-preventing-and-resolving-conflict-pacific%E2%80%9D-canty.
9. Marian Hobbs, *Being Faithful Witness to Our Friends Peace Testimony: Serving God in a Changing World* (London and Philadelphia: Friends World Committee for Consultation, 2004), 9.
10. Nozizwe Madlala-Routledge, "Quaker Values in South Africa's Struggle," Salter Lecture, Britain Yearly Meeting, July 24, 2021. https://quakersocialists.org.uk/2021/06/20/salter-lecture-2021-quaker-values-in-south-africas-struggle/

11. United States tax law defines a category of charitable organizations, called 501 c 3 organizations from the section of the federal tax code. They may engage in education about public issues and support non-partisan ballot measures or referenda but must avoid direct support or lobbying of elected officials. Depending on their individual income tax situation, individuals who contribute money to such organizations may use those contributions to reduce their federal and state income taxes. AFSC did not want to jeopardize the contributions from individuals who were its primary source of funds. FCNL was established under different regulations as a nonprofit to engage directly in lobbying, but without the ability to receive tax-favored contributions. It now operates with parallel organizations — FCNL and FCNL Education Fund, which is 501 c 3. This is a common solution for many organizations, such as the League of Women Voters, which deal with public policy and the political process.

12. Stephen Collett, *Sixty Years with the UN in New York: A History of the Quaker UN Office* (New York: Quaker United Nations Office, 2007).

13. The United States has not ratified but recognizes and abides by most provisions.

14. We did not seek out the many other people in politics who can be described as "Quaker adjacent" rather than Quaker. They may have Quaker ancestors, attended a Quaker school, married a Quaker and occasionally attended church or meeting, or participated in a meeting for a few years as a spiritual seeker, but are not members nor long-time regular participants. Their actions and values, of course, may well reflect Quaker influences.

15. In the United States, local boards that are independent of other governments operate most state-funded or common schools. There are more than 10,000 such school districts,

some setting policy for districts of a couple hundred students and others for districts with tens of thousands. Nobody will ever doubt the maxim "all politics is local" after they have attended a school board meeting that deals with changes to curriculum, sports programs, or, in 2021, COVID-19 rules.

16. Catherine West and Andy Hull, *Faith in Politics: A Testimony to Equality*, 2017 Swarthmore Lecture (London: Quaker Books, 2017), 21, 17.
17. Vallentine and Jones, "Quakers in Politics," 43, 36.
18. Vallentine and Jones, "Quakers in Politics," 19.
19. Lon Fendall, "Evangelical Quakers and Public Policy," in Paul N. Anderson and Howard Macy, eds., *Truth's Bright Embrace: Essays and Poems in Honor of Arthur O. Roberts* (Newberg, OR: George Fox University, 1996), https://digitalcommons.georgefox.edu/truths_bright/19/
20. There are theological similarities among more evangelical Quakers, Methodists, and the Salvation Army (which once published a book titled *George Fox: The Red Hot Quaker*).
21. Marian Hobbs "A Peaceful World: Haw Can We Make It So?" New Zealand Quaker Lecture 2016) https://quakers.nz/sites/default/files/documents/Quaker-Lecture-2016-Marion%20Hobbs.pdf
22. Vallentine notes that Laurie Wilkinson, a Quaker Senator from Western Australia from 1966 to 1974, fund it much easier to speak out and raise issues as an Opposition backbencher than when the Australian Labour Party was in power as backbenchers were then expected to do what they were told.
23. Vallentine and Jones, 40.
24. Phil Caroom and Jim Rose, "Reinvesting in Justice," *Friends Journal*, Sept 1, 2021. https://www.friendsjournal.org/reinvesting-in-justice/
25. Parker Palmer, *Healing the Heart of Democracy: The Courage*

to Create a Politics Worthy of the Human Spirit (San Francisco: Jossey-Bass, 2011), 43.

26. Palmer, *Healing the Heart of Democracy*, 14.
27. Hobbs, *Being Faithful Witness*, 7.

About the Authors

Margery Post Abbott and Carl Abbott are members of Multnomah Meeting in Portland, Oregon, USA, and the authors of *Quakerism: The Basics* (2021). Before turning to writing and teaching about the Society of Friends, Marge managed a medical research lab at the University of Chicago, directed maritime facilities planning for the Port of Portland, and served on the Oregon Ocean Policy Advisory Committee. Her books include *To Be Broken and Tender: A Quaker Theology for Today* (2010), *Walk Humbly, Serve Boldly: Modern Friends as Everyday Prophets* (2018), and *A Theological Perspective on Quaker Lobbying* (2021). Carl has retired from teaching history and city planning at Portland State University in five decades (but not fifty years), as well as holding visiting appointments at the University of Oregon and George Washington University. He has published several books on the history of American cities and on the social context of science fiction. Recent titles include *Imagining Urban Futures: Cities in Science Fiction and What We Might Learn from Them* (2016) and *City Planning: A Very Short Introduction* (2020). They recommend workspaces on two separate floors when collaborating from home. They are happy to respond to comments and queries at marge.quaker@gmail.com and abbottc@pdx.edu.

Also in this series

Quaker Roots and Branches
John Lampen

Quaker Roots and Branches explores what Quakers call their 'testimonies' – the interaction of inspiration, faith and action to bring change in the world. It looks at Quaker concerns around the sustainability of the planet, peace and war, punishment, and music and the arts in the past and today. It stresses the continuity of their witness over three hundred and sixty-five years as well as their openness to change and development.

Telling the Truth about God
Rhiannon Grant

Telling the truth about God without excluding anyone is a challenge to the Quaker community. Drawing on the author's academic research into Quaker uses of religious language and her teaching to Quaker and academic groups, Rhiannon Grant aims to make accessible some key theological and philosophical insights. She explains that Quakers might sound vague but are actually making clear and creative theological claims.

What Do Quakers Believe?
Geoffrey Durham

Geoffrey Durham answers the crucial question 'What do Quakers believe?' clearly, straightforwardly and without jargon. In the process he introduces a unique religious group whose impact and influence in the world is far greater than their numbers suggest. *What Do Quakers Believe?* is a friendly, direct and accessible toe-in-the-water book for readers who have often wondered who these Quakers are, but have never quite found out.

CHRISTIAN ALTERNATIVE
BOOKS

THE NEW OPEN SPACES

Throughout the two thousand years of Christian tradition there have been, and still are, groups and individuals that exist in the margins and upon the edge of faith. But in Christianity's contrapuntal history it has often been these outcasts and pioneers that have forged contemporary orthodoxy out of former radicalism as belief evolves to engage with and encompass the ever-changing social and scientific realities. Real faith lies not in the comfortable certainties of the Orthodox, but somewhere in a half-glimpsed hinterland on the dirt track to Emmaus, where the Death of God meets the Resurrection, where the supernatural Christ meets the historical Jesus, and where the revolution liberates both the oppressed and the oppressors.

Welcome to Christian Alternative... a space at the edge where the light shines through.
If you have enjoyed this book, why not tell other readers by posting a review on your preferred book site.

Recent bestsellers from Christian Alternative are:

Bread Not Stones
The Autobiography of An Eventful Life
Una Kroll
The spiritual autobiography of a truly remarkable woman
and a history of the struggle for ordination in the Church of
England.
Paperback: 978-1-78279-804-0 ebook: 978-1-78279-805-7

The Quaker Way
A Rediscovery
Rex Ambler
Although fairly well known, Quakerism is not well understood.
The purpose of this book is to explain how Quakerism works as
a spiritual practice.
Paperback: 978-1-78099-657-8 ebook: 978-1-78099-658-5

Blue Sky God
The Evolution of Science and Christianity
Don MacGregor
Quantum consciousness, morphic fields and blue-sky
thinking about God and Jesus the Christ.
Paperback: 978-1-84694-937-1 ebook: 978-1-84694-938-8

Celtic Wheel of the Year
Tess Ward
An original and inspiring selection of prayers combining
Christian and Celtic Pagan traditions, and interweaving their
calendars into a single pattern of prayer for every morning
and night of the year.
Paperback: 978-1-90504-795-6

Christian Atheist
Belonging without Believing
Brian Mountford
Christian Atheists don't believe in God but miss him: especially
the transcendent beauty of his music, language, ethics, and
community.
Paperback: 978-1-84694-439-0 ebook: 978-1-84694-929-6

Compassion Or Apocalypse?
A Comprehensible Guide to the Thoughts of René Girard
James Warren
How René Girard changes the way we think about God and the
Bible, and its relevance for our apocalypse-threatened world.
Paperback: 978-1-78279-073-0 ebook: 978-1-78279-072-3

Diary Of A Gay Priest
The Tightrope Walker
Rev. Dr. Malcolm Johnson
Full of anecdotes and amusing stories, but the Church is still a
dangerous place for a gay priest.
Paperback: 978-1-78279-002-0 ebook: 978-1-78099-999-9

Do You Need God?
Exploring Different Paths to Spirituality Even For Atheists
Rory J.Q. Barnes
An unbiased guide to the building blocks of spiritual belief.
Paperback: 978-1-78279-380-9 ebook: 978-1-78279-379-3

Readers of ebooks can buy or view any of these bestsellers by clicking on the live link in the title. Most titles are published in paperback and as an ebook. Paperbacks are available in traditional bookshops. Both print and ebook formats are available online.

Find more titles and sign up to our readers' newsletter at
http://www.johnhuntpublishing.com/christianity
Follow us on Facebook at
https://www.facebook.com/ChristianAlternative